Is This Woman Really Me?

A Memoir

Arwa Aboud

Is This Woman Really Me? A Memoir

Published by Arwa Ghali Publishing

Printed in the United States of America

First Edition, 2026

ISBN 979-8-9947658-1-4 (paperback)

ISBN 979-8-9947658-0-7 (hardcover)

Some names and identifying details have been changed to protect the privacy of individuals.

This is a work of memoir. The events and conversations in this book have been recreated from the author's memory and personal recollection. Others may remember events differently.

Cover photograph: AI-enhanced portrait of the author.

For my family

Who gave us the best education and never let us feel the weight of need. Who shielded us from the ugliness of the world and built a life where we never had to ask for what we deserved.

Who kept a roof over my head when the nights were at their darkest, and whose love held me up when I had nothing left to stand on.

And who never once asked how old I was before deciding I still needed them. You had my back when I was a child. You had my back when I was a mother. You have my back still.

That kind of love does not have an expiration date. I know because I felt it every single time I needed it most.

For my children

You were children who should have known only softness. Instead, you knew fear. Humiliation. Uncertainty. Not because of anything you did. Because of choices I made trying to survive.

My son, at sixteen years old, you put your body between me and danger. You were a child protecting your mother. No child should ever have to do that. And yet you did it without hesitation. You saved my life at the cost of your own innocence. I will never stop being in awe of you.

My daughters, you grew up in the shadow of a storm you didn't create. You endured what no child should endure. And still you became kind. Strong. Whole. Not despite what you lived through. Because of whom you already were inside it.

You didn't just survive my story. You became the best parts of it.

I owe you more than words. But I start here.

And for Diaa

You were never supposed to leave this soon. But then again, neither was the light.

Your name meant light in the language we shared. You didn't just carry that meaning you became it. You were the air I forgot I needed until I couldn't breathe without you. The peace I didn't know existed until you handed it to me. Everything good. Everything real. Everything mine.

You showed me a love so unconditional, so quietly extraordinary, that I spent years convinced it only existed in movie theaters. Then you walked in.

You made me believe I deserved it.

I am still learning that you were right. I think I will be learning that for the rest of my life.

Contents

Is this Woman Really Me

The Beginning

(Prologue – Identity, Survival, Reflection)

Before you turn the page, I want you to pause. Take a breath.

Think of the version of yourself that the world sees, the one that smiles, shows up, keeps going. Now think of the version no one ever asks about. This book lives in the space between those two women.

For years, people told me I was strong. They called me a survivor. A role model. A hero. I laughed every time. Heroes, I believed, were fearless. Certain. Unbreakable. I was none of those things. I was simply surviving, putting one foot in front of the other, because stopping was never a choice. But the words kept coming. From friends. From family. From strangers who knew only fragments of my story. They saw something in me that I could not see in myself. So, I began asking a question I had avoided my entire life: Who am I, really? When I look in the mirror, I see an ordinary woman. Someone you could pass on the street and never remember. A face that hides its storms well. And yet, I carry them all. I survived twenty-two years of abuse, the kind that doesn't always leave bruises, but always leaves doubt. Abuse that teaches you to apologize for things you didn't do. Abuse that slowly convinces you that love means erasing yourself. I left everything to survive. I lost everything again. I rebuilt from less than three hundred dollars in a country where fear came wrapped in paperwork and waiting. And then I fell in love with the man I was meant to grow old with. Instead, I watched him disappear. Cancer does not take someone all at once. It takes them in pieces. Over months. Day by day. I learned the weight of helplessness as I stood beside the strongest man I knew and watched his body betray him. I memorized the sound of hospital machines, the shape of pain in his eyes, the silence that followed conversations we would never finish. I held his hand while the future we planned quietly unraveled. Still, I kept going. Not because I was brave. But because survival does not ask for courage. It demands it. This book is not about staying. It is about leaving. Breaking. Healing. Becoming. It is about the question every woman who survives eventually asks herself: Is this woman really me? And maybe, if you're honest, you've asked it too.

Chapter 1: Childhood and Privilege

If my story feels distorted or scattered, please forgive me. The truth is, I can't always remember the exact order of events. Trauma doesn't keep time.

Most of us think our story begins when we grow older, when life tests us, breaks us, or forces us to rise. But the truth is, our story begins much earlier than we imagine. It begins in the quiet moments of childhood, when events that seem small and insignificant leave invisible marks on our hearts. Those moments shape who we become, how we love, how we trust, and how we face the world.

The memories start to run like a movie playing too fast to capture. I go back as far as memory will take me, searching my childhood, trying to figure out when my story truly began.

My father was a diplomat stationed in Amman, Jordan, beginning in 1979. He worked at the Arab League as one of Iraq's official representatives. What did that mean for us? It meant privilege. Access. Prestige.

We attended one of the best private schools in the country, so exclusive that even the King of Jordan's son, Prince Ali, was one of my classmates.

The campus stretched across an entire city block. There was a vast soccer field, a theater with velvet-covered seats, a proper stage, backstage dressing rooms, and a professional lighting system controlled from a dedicated room at the back. The King himself visited twice a year, and when he did, the entire campus held its breath.

Even our school buses were different, always a Mercedes-Benz. A fleet the King helped sustain by donating two brand-new buses every year. I remember watching those shiny buses pull up in front of our house every morning with childlike awe. His charisma seemed to light up the air around him. Every time he visited, I felt the same urge: to break past the crowd and run toward him, just to be near that kind of power, that kind of magic.

Our uniforms, however, were hideous, dark dresses with stiff collars. But they set us apart from public-school students. We didn't realize it then, but we were growing up inside a world of extraordinary privilege, one that followed us everywhere, even beyond the school gates.

Each of us was issued a diplomatic ID, an invisible shield that meant no airport lines, no searched bags, and a different kind of smile from the world, one laced with respect, deference, even envy.

I was the youngest in my family and the only daughter, spoiled, yes, showered with gifts and attention. My father gave me a tenderness my brothers never knew. And yet, even then, I often felt like the adult in the room.

I would march into my older brother's classroom, ask his teachers how he was doing, and carry their reports home. I was a child playing guardian, wearing a crown of invisible responsibility, one I wouldn't fully understand until much later.

My mother loved us fiercely, but her love spoke a language I didn't always understand, especially as a child. She gave everything she had, but her world was built on duty and sacrifice, shaped by generations of women who measured love through labor and acts of service, not tenderness.

She was always in motion, cooking, cleaning, folding laundry, ironing shirts, sweeping floors. Her hands never stopped. She never painted her nails or blow-dried her hair. In her world, self-care was indulgence, even wasteful. She hadn't been taught to nurture herself, so she didn't know how to teach us.

Still, I loved her with all my heart. She gave us everything within her reach: warm meals, clean clothes, a spotless home. That was her love, quiet, constant, unwavering service.

But there were no bedtime stories. No painted toenails. No whispered secrets between mother and daughter. No hugs and kisses. No spoken emotions.

I don't remember her laughing, not really. Her face was always etched with seriousness, her eyes fixed on the next task.

I remember one moment vividly. I was in first grade, preparing for a dictation exam. I wanted her to read the paragraph aloud to me, the way I'd seen other mothers do. Instead, she said, "Read the first line, hide it, then write it."

Just that. No hand-holding. No encouragement. Just a method. A system.

It wasn't cruelty. It was all she knew.

And maybe that's when I started to believe I had to figure out life on my own.

Our school was Islamic, so I never had Christian friends and knew nothing about Christianity beyond what was taught in textbooks. Religion wasn't something we could question or even discuss. We were taught to keep our distance. No mingling. No curiosity.

But while the world around me drew sharp lines between people, my mind wandered past them.

I remember looking up at the night sky as a little girl. It felt darker then, fuller somehow, maybe it truly had more stars, or maybe that's just how childhood sees the world. After evening school events, the drive home felt magical, quiet roads, cooler air, and skies that looked deeper. The darkness felt softer. The stars, brighter.

I'd press my forehead against the car window and watch the city drift by in lights and shadows. My eyes would catch the glowing windows of apartment buildings, and I'd wonder:

Who lives behind those glowing windows?

Which of them is the hero in their story… and which of us are just the blurry background?

Summers were a passport to elsewhere. One year we'd go to Iraq, the next to Turkey or Bulgaria. We drove through forests and up winding mountain roads, spent months by the Black Sea, sun-kissed, barefoot, free.

But visiting Iraq was different. The preparation began months in advance. My parents would spend weeks buying gifts for every relative on both sides of the family.

Our arrival was never quiet. Anticipation stirred the streets, whispers of our return moving from house to house before we even landed. Neighbors would gather, children would chase after our car, relatives would stand waiting outside just to catch a glimpse of us pulling in. Even those who weren't related joined the crowd, just to witness our return.

It felt like a celebration. But it was also a reminder that we were different, that we didn't quite belong.

Iraq was at war with Iran. Every family knew someone on the front lines: a father, a son, a husband, a brother.

But not us.

We were spared. We were safe. And even as a child, I knew that kind of safety came at a cost. Still, we were outsiders.

We came only once a year, parachuting into lives that had continued without us. Our cousins shared memories, inside jokes, scars we couldn't see but felt in every silence. They had lived through things we hadn't. They spoke a language of hardship we didn't yet understand.

My parents, though, belonged. Iraq was their home, their past, their heart. They had friends there, a shared history, roots that ran deep. For them, going back was never a question, it was the plan.

What began as a four-year diplomatic post in Jordan stretched into twenty years, but their dream never changed. Iraq was the end goal. Jordan was just a pause.

What they didn't see, what they couldn't see, was that we, their children, had grown into a different dream.

Jordan wasn't a stopover for us. It was the only home we had ever known.

Returning to Iraq wasn't our longing. It was theirs.

We didn't belong there. We weren't forged by war. We hadn't learned the same kind of resilience. Our hopes were softer, simpler, more naïve and we were too young to realize just how vulnerable that made us.

My parents gave everything they could to support our extended family back in Iraq. My father helped his brothers build their houses. He paid for their children's education out of his own salary. He gave generously, without hesitation, believing that family meant forever.

But when financial hardship came knocking, all of that was forgotten. The gratitude faded. The kindness disappeared.

It is startling how quickly people turn their backs when the money runs out.

Everything my parents had done, the years of support, the sacrifices, the giving without limits vanished the moment they no longer had anything left to give.

As if love had an expiration date.

As if generosity carried no weight once the money stopped flowing.

I watched them pour themselves into their families, only to be discarded like old furniture when fortunes changed.

And yet, somehow, I followed the same path. Giving without limits. Caring too deeply. Believing that love and goodness would be enough to make people stay.

I thought that if I loved hard enough, helped enough, sacrificed enough, I could hold the world together.

Maybe it was because that's what I saw growing up: love as service, loyalty as obligation, forgiveness as silence. It was the only model I knew and for a long time, I had no reason to believe another one existed.

She Was the Light. I Became the Shadow.

I was nine years old when my sister was born, and everything changed.

She was breathtaking, blue-green eyes, golden hair, the kind of beauty that turned heads even as a baby.

I had brown eyes and dark hair. Simple. Ordinary. Forgettable in comparison.

For nine years, I had been the baby of the family, the center of attention, the one they adored without effort or competition. And then, suddenly, I wasn't.

Her arrival didn't just make me an older sister; it quietly took away the role that had once made me feel special. I didn't know how to name it then, but something in me dimmed.

Mental health wasn't something anyone talked about back then. No one considered how a shift like that could leave a mark on a child's sense of worth.

At the same time, my mother started working at the Iraqi Embassy in Jordan, which, coincidentally, sat just across the street from my school.

Every afternoon, after classes ended, I'd cross the road alone and wait for her in the embassy lobby. It became a new routine, a new kind of quiet.

That job brought us into a different world: ambassadors' wives, women's union members, and circles of royalty. The women my mother spent time with changed, and so did she.

Her world began to expand, while mine somehow grew smaller.

She was now working among prime ministers and cabinet members. She began to dress up, color her hair, and get regular blowouts. She was invited to elegant receptions, official dinners, and glamorous events. There was a glow about her, a new energy, a version of her I had never seen before. With her petite frame and her new wardrobe, she transformed completely.

My mother and my baby sister became the center of attention the picture everyone noticed: the beautiful mother and her angelic little girl.

And me?

I started to disappear.

I began binge-eating quietly, secretly, often without understanding why. The weight came quickly, and so did the judgment. I became the chubby girl, mocked at school, teased at home.

They chastised me for eating, but no one offered a hand, a plan, or even kindness. Just shame.

It was the 1980s. Clothing options were limited, especially if you didn't fit the mold. Children's stores didn't carry my size. Women's stores weren't meant for little girls. I found myself wedged somewhere in between, trying to shrink inside oversized dresses that were never made for me.

Each ill-fitting outfit was more than uncomfortable fabric; it was a reminder that I didn't belong.

Not in my body.

Not in my clothes.

Not even in my own story.

As we grew, tragedy scorched our childhood in a way none of us could have imagined. My sister suffered a terrible burn when boiling water spilled across her back while she was playing. I was there in the car as we rushed her to the emergency room. Her skin peeled in front of me while I held her. Just open flesh and unbearable pain. She couldn't move, couldn't cry loudly enough to match the agony in her body.

For over a month, she lay in the burn unit, sleeping on her stomach, her back exposed. No bandages, just a sterile sheet stretched across a metal frame that hovered above her body, while nurses applied thick layers of burn cream to prevent infection. Her skin was too wounded to touch, too fragile to turn.

Each day, I sat beside her, watching as new skin slowly, painfully began to form a miracle born out of trauma.

The doctor said, "She's young. But for her skin to regain any uniform tone, she'll need to tan deeply. Only then will it blend, and there will be no trace of the burn."

So, my siblings and I were enrolled in an exclusive country club, the kind reserved for the elite. The pool sparkled. The sun was merciless. Joy seemed to hang in the air for everyone but me.

I wasn't there to swim. I was there to watch over her.

In the strict culture my parents were raised in, women were not allowed to smile in public, let alone show skin. I was a teenager, but my sister, still very young, was allowed to wear a tiny bathing suit with minimal coverage because it was medically necessary. An exception for healing.

My brothers, of course, were boys, protected by male privilege and the freedom that came with it.

While they swam and laughed, carefree and glowing, I stood fully clothed beneath the unforgiving summer sky. My clothes clung to me, soaked with sweat. I burned in silence while they bathed in sunlight.

I was the silent guardian. The shadow beside the fun. Trying to avoid the stares of people who looked at me as if I were a spectacle, an oddity under the same sun that everyone else seemed to belong to.

That summer, they tanned.

I blistered.

From that day on, my sister was granted freedoms I never knew. Privileges bloomed around her like second chances, unspoken allowances, quiet indulgences. While she healed, I learned to shrink. She became the fragile one, the precious one. And I became the strong one, expected to carry the weight, to never ask for more. I was the helper, the caretaker, the shadow, the one who didn't need special treatment. And without realizing it, I learned how to disappear, how to mute my needs to keep the peace.

To this day, my sister speaks her mind without hesitation, never afraid of judgment. She says what she feels, and the world adjusts around her. But me? I spent a lifetime trying to keep everyone happy, quiet, careful, and

Chapter 2: When love was a dream

When I started college, my brother A.G and I had one year of overlap. He was studying political science, and we were on the same campus. That first year was the most fun I'd ever had. We skipped classes, went to parties, and laughed until our stomachs hurt. For the first time in my life, I felt free, light, unburdened, and a little reckless.

But beneath the fun was a path I hadn't chosen.

I had enrolled in dental school, mostly to meet my family's expectations. It didn't take long to realize I wasn't cut out for it. I couldn't handle the blood, the pressure. The day we were asked to dissect a mouse, I fainted. Right then, I knew, this wasn't me. This wasn't my future.

So, I pivoted. I changed majors and entered pharmacy. It was grueling: long hours in labs, endless pages of science, precision, pressure. But something in me clicked. I could do this. I was built for this kind of challenge.

Toward the end of my first year, I made a new friend in my pharmacy class. Not just a classmate, not just a friend, but someone who would leave an imprint on my life for as long as I live.

R.H was tiny but full of energy and charm. In many ways, she felt like my mirror, except sometimes it seemed like she resented me more than she cared for me. She had a way of complimenting and criticizing in the same breath, leaving me constantly unsure of where I stood with her.

She knew my ex-husband from high school and spoke about him often, this mysterious friend who was handsome, smart, wealthy, and came from a very good family. He was studying to become a dentist. For a while, I honestly thought she was making him up. I laughed once and told her I wished I could meet this secret friend, since we never seemed to see him anywhere.

Then one day, as we were walking to class, I spotted an incredibly handsome man crossing the courtyard with a friend who was just as striking. I leaned closer to R.H and whispered, half-joking, "He's so handsome."

Without missing a beat, she lit up.

"Oh, it's him! "My friend I told you about," she said, her eyes sparkling with something I couldn't quite name. Then she began listing his qualities one after another, as if reading from a résumé. He was her mysterious friend, the one she always spoke about with an air of intrigue and quiet ownership, as if he belonged partly to her world, not mine.

She called them over immediately. She knew them both; they lived in her neighborhood. And just like that, the space between us vanished.

We began talking casually about school, our majors, and where we were from. When it was my turn, I said, "I'm Iraqi."

That's when it happened.

He looked at me, really looked at me, and something unspoken passed between us. His eyes locked onto mine and the world around us softened. There was a stillness in that gaze, like everything paused. I paused. I held his gaze and forgot what I was saying. Forgot where I was.

For a moment, there was no one else. Not even R.H standing beside him. Just us, caught in some silent, magnetic current.

Then she nudged me, and time resumed.

But I already knew something had shifted. And nothing would ever be quite the same again.

Butterflies? No.

A whole swarm.

He looked like James Dean, cool, confident, untouchable. His friend was just as handsome, but he didn't carry the same gravity, the same invisible pull that drew me toward him. His friend was studying civil engineering. My ex-husband was in dental school.

I was smitten.

And just like that, my love story began.

Dating wasn't allowed, not publicly, not openly. One-on-one time with a boy could ruin a girl's reputation forever. So, we moved in packs, spoke in glances, and danced around suspicion. It was a careful choreography of youthful desire and cultural restraint.

He was an Adiga, part of an ethnic group descended from the Circassians, driven out of Russia during the Hundred Years' War. Adigas were proud, wealthy, almost royal by association, having served in the royal court and acted as confidants to the royal family. Their community was tight-knit and insular, bound by heritage and unspoken rules. Strangers were unwelcome in their circle.

So, when I found myself falling for one of them, it felt both impossible and intoxicating. The crush was more than just attraction; it was a form of validation. That someone like him, with his pedigree, his presence, could fall for me, felt like I had broken through an invisible barrier.

Chapter 3: Echoes and Gut Feelings

Red Flags

They rise up the way they always do, uninvited, somewhere between the highway exit and the morning light, fragments of a life I lived so fully that I sometimes forget it wasn't someone else's story.

Red flags weren't a concept when I was a young woman. No one taught us how to recognize manipulation or narcissism. There were no conversations about emotional abuse, no language for it. Whatever men did was deemed acceptable. They were men. They couldn't possibly be wrong. And if you dared to question it, the answer was always the same:

"All men are like that. You just have to adapt. Learn how to live with it."

But women… we were given a gift. A quiet, powerful voice tucked deep inside us: gut instinct. And mine has never failed me.

My gut feeling was like a compass, whispering truths long before the facts surfaced. I didn't always listen to it, though, or know how to.

My sister M.G used to say that whenever I said, "I have a feeling," she would feel a knot twist in her stomach. Because more often than not, I was right.

I had a gut feeling when I met my ex-husband. But I chose to ignore it.

Just days after meeting him, something deep inside me whispered: He's not the one.

That was my intuition, soft but steady. I felt it like a quiet warning echoing in my chest. But he was persistent. Persuasive. He wove himself into my life so effortlessly, so skillfully, that I began to doubt the voice inside me.

He was handsome, painfully handsome. Smart, too. And that combination blurred the edges of my judgment.

I let myself fall.

He became my tutor. We spent hours together, buried in textbooks and quiet laughter. He made me feel seen, wanted, and admired. One day, as we studied, he casually told me that his closest friend had a crush on me too. But then he added, with a possessive grin, "I told him, you're too late. She's mine."

And just like that, I was claimed.

Now imagine that girl, full of insecurities, self-doubt, and a fragile sense of worth, suddenly admired and desired by two handsome men. And claimed by the one she already had a tremendous crush on. It felt surreal.

Pharmacy school and dental school shared the same entrance, and my ex-husband was always there waiting for me before my early morning classes, catching me between lectures, reappearing again in the afternoon. My inexperienced heart mistook his constant presence for love. I didn't know the difference between affection and obsession. Not yet.

He asked me to remove my glasses whenever we walked through the campus center. Years later, he admitted why: he didn't want me to recognize people who waved at me. He wanted them to think I was ignoring them. Eventually they stopped waving. And I lost almost all the friends I had made in my first year of college.

It was control disguised as vanity.

When he went out with friends, he'd drive to my neighborhood and sit in his car for hours, just to watch me through our apartment windows.

Stalker behavior?

Yes.

But back then, I thought it was devotion. He'd bring over food so we could eat the same thing. He called it romance, and I believed him.

The first time I visited his family, the illusion cracked. There were two old cars parked in front of their house, both undrivable. Their so-called "villa" was a modest three-bedroom, one-and-a-half-bath townhome. This wasn't the world I had imagined. It was nothing like R.H had described.

We were from different socioeconomic backgrounds.

But by then, I was too far gone, blinded by what I thought was love. And I wasn't shallow. Money didn't matter to me. Love conquers all… or so I believed.

The signs that we belonged together felt too unusual to ignore. Our college ID numbers were almost identical: 914056 and 934056. Both of our grandmothers, on my mother's side and his father's side, shared the same first name. It didn't feel like coincidence; it felt like fate.

A cosmic wink. Proof that the universe had conspired to bring us together.

But in hindsight… maybe the universe wasn't drawing hearts. Maybe it was sending warnings, and I read them all wrong.

We spent all our free time together, every hour between lectures, every weekend, every pause in our schedules and everyone knew we were it. The couple people envied. He consumed my world.

Everything began and ended with him. My thoughts, my choices, the rhythm of my days revolved around his presence. I didn't just love him, I surrendered to him, piece by piece, until there was nothing left untouched by his orbit. I gave up my own world willingly, believing that being part of his was enough. But somewhere in that exchange, I lost myself.

While others were discovering who they were, making friends, building memories, finding joy in ordinary moments, I was shrinking. I didn't get to know my classmates. I didn't learn how to belong anywhere outside of him. My life became a quiet repetition of waiting, pleasing, and existing in the shadow of his expectations.

In 1993, my father relocated to Egypt, while my mother stayed behind to continue her post at the embassy. The separation made sense. He needed time to settle in, and she was committed to her role.

Years passed. By 1997, it had been almost three years since we met, and everyone had no doubt we would get married once we graduated. That year, my mother was offered a transfer to Cairo, same job, different country. She accepted without hesitation.

By then, my ex-husband had graduated and was working as a dentist with the Royal Medical Services. I still had one year left in school.

My family, though reluctant, was open to the idea of him proposing. They weren't going to leave me alone in Jordan unless we were formally engaged. You'd think that after being inseparable for three years, he'd jump at the chance to make our relationship official.

But he didn't. He said he wasn't ready.

That should have been the sign. That was the sign. So, I ended things.

Around that same time, a friend of a friend tried to introduce me to her son in England. Word spread that I might get engaged soon. That's when everything shifted from charm to obsession.

He began parking outside our apartment at night, his car becoming a shadow I could no longer ignore. Sometimes he sat there for hours, watching, waiting. Other times, he showed up unannounced, pleading with my mother to let him see me.

"I brought her this," he'd say, holding up a sandwich. "She needs to eat. I want us to eat the same thing."

What might sound unsettling to others felt like love to me. I didn't recognize it as control disguised as devotion. Every moment he wasn't working, he kept himself tethered to my life from the outside.

The night before my family was set to leave, he showed up at our door, charming, composed, disarming. He spoke to my father with poise and confidence, and somehow, he won him over. Just like that, he had their blessing. We were engaged.

My family left everything behind for us, the furniture and the appliances, so we wouldn't have to worry about anything. They even promised they would return for the engagement party, which they paid for entirely. It all happened so fast. My father, who had sworn over and over that he would rather see me dead than married to a Jordanian, suddenly gave his blessing. We went from "not in a million years" to "you have our blessing."

Sometimes I wonder: was he really that persuasive? Or was it just easier for everyone?

I pull into the parking lot and sit for a moment before getting out of the car. The engine goes quiet. The road is behind me now, and so are the memories, tucked back into the place where they live, somewhere between my ribs and my breath.

I catch a glimpse of myself in the side mirror. The morning light filters through the windshield, soft but unforgiving, and for a moment it lands squarely on my face.

I freeze. I share the same face with that woman. The same eyes. The same skin. The same frame. But something about her feels unfamiliar.

Her eyes look tired, not from lack of sleep, but from carrying too much. Her expression is composed, yet her spirit trembles beneath the surface, like a cracked vase holding water just long enough to pretend it's whole.

I share her DNA, her story, her past. But I can feel that something inside her is breaking, slowly, quietly, the way glass gives in before it shatters.

And as I stare, caught between recognition and disbelief, a thought rises, gentle but piercing:

Is this woman really me?

Chapter 4: Surviving and Betrayal

How did I get here? Is it my fault? Where did I go wrong? Could I have done things differently? Why did I stay? How blind was I to the truth of the abuse I was living in? Was I sick, or just broken, to endure it for so long? How did I let him destroy me piece by piece? Where was my self-respect?

These were the questions that haunted me, living like shadows in the back of my mind from the moment I escaped that cycle of abuse. They didn't arrive all at once. They accumulated, one by one, the way damage does, quietly, until the weight of them became impossible to ignore.

When I applied for asylum in the United States, one of the requirements was attending group therapy. Eight sessions. A circle of eight women, each of us carrying invisible bruises, memories that refused to fade, and a shared fear of being seen too closely.

We were from different worlds, different languages, ages, and faiths. Some had fled war. Others had escaped marriages, homes, or families that had once promised safety. But once we sat in that circle, none of that mattered. Pain has a way of translating itself without words.

In those sessions, the air always felt heavy, filled with the quiet ache of stories we couldn't fully tell. Sometimes the silence spoke louder than any confession. A hand on a knee, a nod across the circle, a tear wiped quickly before it fell those became our language.

And despite our differences, we were all asking the same questions I had been asking myself since the day I escaped. In that circle, I finally found some answers.

No, I wasn't crazy.

Abusive people don't simply hurt you. They study you. They learn your fears, your hopes, the exact words that make you crumble, and the ones that make you stay. They trap you in a vicious, calculated cycle that blurs the line between love and control until you can no longer tell the difference.

They break you piece by piece, then suddenly become the person you fell in love with, the one who smiled softly, who promised forever. They say the right things, do the right things. Apologies. Grand gestures. A touch that feels tender again. For a fleeting moment, they treat you like a queen, and you cling to that version of him as proof that the cruelty was just a mistake, a passing storm.

You start to believe the darkness is temporary, that the real version of him is the loving one. You convince yourself that if you love him enough, stay kind enough, patient enough, maybe that version will stay.

So, you stay.

Looking back now, I see a pattern. Every five years, almost like clockwork, I reached my breaking point. My body would give out before my mind did, the sleepless nights, the quiet tears, the hollow exhaustion that only someone living in survival mode truly understands.

And each time I finally said, "Enough," he came undone. He would come home in tears, collapsing at my feet like a sinner begging for salvation. He kissed my hands, called me his queen, his angel, his reason for breathing. His words spilled out like poetry, desperate and rehearsed, designed to pull me back into orbit.

In those moments, he worshiped me. Not as a woman or a wife, but as a goddess who could redeem him. He brought me my favorite meals, slipped love notes into my purse, flooded my phone with calls just to say he missed me.

It was intoxicating, the way he adored me after the storm. That sudden tenderness, that intensity, felt like proof that love could heal what it had broken.

And each time, I gave in. I mistook his performance for repentance. I mistook obsession for devotion. I clung to the illusion because believing in his change was easier than accepting that he never would.

But the abuse always returned, stronger, sharper, crueler. Each cycle cut deeper than the last. My forgiveness didn't heal him. It fed him. It didn't soften his anger. It sanctioned it. Every time I stayed, I unknowingly gave him permission to break me a little more. I thought love could save him, but all it did was teach him that I would never leave, no matter what he did.

When my family left the country and I was alone with him, everything shifted. The mask fell away. The control that once hid behind charm and apologies turned into entitlement. He began insisting on a sexual relationship. On paper, we were married, just waiting for the official celebration.

But in our world, that celebration wasn't a formality. It was everything. It was the line between honor and disgrace, between a woman and her ruin. It was the moment that transformed a legal contract into something sacred, blessed by family, sealed by community, recognized by God.

Virtue wasn't just a personal value. It was the currency of a woman's worth. It was the fabric that held our entire society together, woven tightly with shame and silence. A woman's honor was never truly her own. It belonged to her family, her tribe, her ancestors. One misstep, one rumor, one whisper could stain generations.

I grew up knowing that my choices didn't just define me. They defined everyone who shared my blood. That weight wasn't just moral. It was cultural, ancestral, suffocating. It wrapped around my throat like an invisible rope, reminding me that my purity was never about me. It was about preserving the illusion of perfection for everyone else.

Yet despite everything I had been taught, despite every warning and every whispered prayer for strength, under my ex-husband's relentless insistence, I gave in. Before the wedding celebration, before the formal blessing of our union, I crossed a line I had been taught to fear with every cell in my body.

I didn't surrender because I didn't care. I surrendered because I was exhausted, worn down by the pressure, the pleading, the guilt disguised as love. Every "if you love me" felt like a trap. Every silence felt like punishment. His persistence was a storm that eroded my resistance grain by grain, until all that was left was compliance.

And when it was over, I carried the shame alone, just as I had been warned I would.

In some parts of our world, a man can kill his sister, his daughter, or his wife in the name of honor, and society barely blinks. That was the weight I lived under. That was the air I breathed.

In our world, dignity was never truly about women. It was about protecting men. Our purity was their pride, our silence, their safety net. Once I gave in, I knew the life I had imagined for myself was already behind me. There would be no dissolving the marriage, no reclaiming my body, my choice, or my voice. By our standards, I was now damaged goods, bound to him not by love, but by shame.

That mindset, that culture, did more than enable him. It emboldened him. It whispered in his ear that no matter what he did, he would be protected. That my virtue was his weapon, my fear his shield. He knew that if I ever tried to break free, he had something more powerful than fists or threats: honor.

And when, after years of emotional warfare and control, I finally found the courage to leave, he reached for that tribal law like a dagger. He told me he would kill me, not in rage, but with cold conviction, as though duty demanded it.

Worse, he said he'd accuse me of adultery. He'd make up stories, paint me as the dishonored wife, the fallen woman. Because in our world, that's all it would take. A single accusation. A single lie. He could walk away with blood on his hands, his pride intact, his conscience clean, while society nodded in approval. Because in our world, a man's word was truth, and a woman's pain was proof of her guilt.

When the fabrications began, when he started spinning tales and planting messages to make them look real, even my son B.S saw it. He saw the messages on my phone, his father's careful web of deceit, the way he twisted conversations into traps, sculpting a story where I was the villain.

And my son B.S knew. He believed it, just like I did. We both believed he was going to kill me. Because in our world, he could.

That night, the night I gave in to him, he revealed exactly who he was. With one smooth gesture, he reached into the ruins of my trust and took everything. The money from the sale of my parents' furniture was gone. The monthly allowance my father had entrusted to me was quietly rerouted to his mother, as if I were merely a messenger in someone else's story.

But he didn't storm in or raise his voice. He didn't have to. He was far too skilled for that. His cruelty wore a mask of calm authority; his control draped in the language of love.

He wrapped his dominance in sweet-sounding concern. "I'm just helping you." "It's for your own good." "You shouldn't worry about these things."

He disguised manipulation as guidance, and over time, he painted me as a fragile woman, too soft, too sentimental, too foolish to manage her own life. And I, craving peace, aching for affection, still tangled in the illusion of safety, handing him the keys to my freedom.

Not in one dramatic moment, but in a hundred quiet ones. Each time I let a decision slide. Each time I stayed silent to keep the peace. Each time I whispered to myself, "He knows better."

My family had left me a car so I could drive to school and work. But some mornings, I'd wake up and find it gone, no note, no explanation. Just an empty driveway and the echo of my own confusion. It wasn't just the car he took. It was the simple belief that anything in my life truly belonged to me.

My mother-in-law I.Z's car wouldn't start, so he took mine without asking. It didn't even occur to him that I might need it too, that I had school, classes, a life of my own waiting beyond the walls of his convenience.

I didn't know how to set boundaries. No one had ever taught me that love and obedience weren't the same thing. I thought love meant sacrifice, that quietness was grace, that compliance was virtue. And every time I tried to speak, just enough to draw a line, to remind him I was still there, I was silenced with labels:

Rude. Disrespectful. Ungrateful.

So, I learned to fold myself smaller. To take up less space. To speak in ways that wouldn't sound like defiance.

I bought my own wedding dress. I took out a bank loan so his family could host the wedding they had promised but failed to fund. I started working before my diploma was even in my hand. And through it all, I whispered to myself: this is love. This is what devoted women do.

When my father sent money so I could buy a safe, reliable car, my ex-husband used it instead to buy me an old Volkswagen Beetle, a far cry from the sleek car I once drove. And it slipped out of his lips without shame: "You are not driving a better car than the one my mother drives."

But I smiled anyway. I told myself it had character. That it was charming. That love wasn't about luxury.

But deep down, I knew. It was never about the car. It was about control, the slow, surgical stripping of autonomy wrapped in the ribbons of tradition.

He insulted my family, mocked their kindness, questioned their worth. But by then, it didn't matter. I had already surrendered my virtue, and in our world, that meant the deal was sealed. I was his now, body, reputation, and name.

So, we swallowed our pride. My mother, my father, and I walked through the motions of celebration, not out of joy, but out of obligation. Honor had chained us even when he had given us nothing to honor. We smiled for photographs that would later feel like evidence of our own surrender, not our happiness.

He disrespected the very people who raised me, questioned their worth, dismissed their sacrifices, yet he relied on them quietly and shamelessly to keep us afloat. When bills piled up, it was my father who paid. When we struggled, it was my mother who sent help. He never thanked them. He never carried the weight.

Responsibility, to him, was a task for others, something to delegate, not something to bear.

Chapter 5: When Love Jumps from the Window

My mother always valued financial security. To her, stability wasn't just comfort. It was protection. She wanted me and my sister M.G to find someone who could give us the luxury of never having to worry, never having to beg, never having to need.

She used to say, "When poverty comes through the door, love jumps out through the window."

Her words were half warning, half prophecy. She had lived enough life to know that affection doesn't always survive hunger, that romance wilts under the weight of unpaid bills and unkept promises.

My sister M.G and I used to roll our eyes, exchange knowing looks, certain that love was stronger than money. We were idealists then, untouched by struggle, convinced that real love could conquer anything.

But we had never known poverty. We had never felt its quiet humiliation, its way of turning tenderness into tension, or its power to strip dignity from a home.

Back then, I thought my mother's words were cynical. Now, I understand they were born from experience, the kind of wisdom you don't read in books but learn from surviving.

After the wedding, reality hit like a slap, sharp, cold, and unapologetic. The romance faded faster than the echo of the vows.

We had four hundred dollars to survive the month. After rent, only two hundred remained, and that, somehow, had to become everything.

You'd think that kind of scarcity would pull two people closer, make them a team. But instead, it revealed the truth: I was the team.

The day after the wedding ceremony, I had to sell whatever gold I had just to survive. We lived off it for a while. A couple of months after the wedding, the gold was gone, and I was left with nothing but the smallest wedding band I owned.

While I was selling everything that had value just to keep us afloat, my ex-husband walked into an electronics store one afternoon, his eyes glowing the way mine used to when I imagined a future with him. Without a word, he bought himself a gaming computer on an installment plan, one hundred and twenty dollars a month. No conversation. No plan. Just impulse.

That left us with eighty dollars. Eighty dollars to eat, to pay bills, to put gas in our cars, and to exist.

I remember standing in the kitchen that night, staring at the grocery list I'd written on a torn envelope, realizing that everything I added meant something else had to go. He sat in the next room, the screen flashing across his face like it was lighting his purpose. I could hear the soft clicks of the keyboard, the sound of a man escaping into a world where responsibility didn't exist.

Our time off was divided into only two activities. We either spent it at my mother-in-law I.Z's house, or at home where he was lost behind that monitor while I was lost inside my own head, doing math, doing damage control, doing everything except feeling loved.

One day, I decided to stop talking. I matched his silence, his carelessness, and spent time in front of the same screen, just to see if he'd notice. He did, but not with awareness. He sulked and pouted like a child who had been denied attention.

I tried to explain. I tried to use words instead of silence, to show him how small I had become, how invisible I felt inside our home, how I wanted him to spend time with me and not with the screen. I spoke softly, believing we were equals, partners.

But instead of listening, he struck me. The back of his hand cut across my face, sudden, deliberate, final.

I was punished for daring to speak. For holding up a mirror he didn't want to see.

The sting wasn't only on my skin. It burned through everything I thought I knew about love. Because in that moment, love shattered. Respect vanished. And I understood: I wasn't a partner. I was property that had spoken out of turn.

And still, I stayed. Because fear had settled into my bones. Because honor had locked the doors. Because I had nowhere else to go.

When I told my mother, I expected outrage, protection, something. Instead, she asked, "What did you do to make him hit you?"

Her question hurt more than the slap. That's how deeply men were protected. How easily women were blamed.

My mother-in-law I.Z defended him too. "You provoked him," she said.

My family tried to intervene. My father's intention was to take me home. But my insecurities surfaced, and the blame eventually shifted to me for provoking him. When conflict stays between two married people, it can sometimes be repaired quietly. But when families are brought in, the fight no longer belongs to the couple. It breeds resentment on all sides, and reconciliation becomes humiliating because it happens under the weight of everyone else's judgment.

After that, my parents stopped involving themselves in my relationship. Not because they stopped caring, but because I stopped sharing. Shame and guilt have a way of building walls even between the people who love you most.

I was married to my ex-husband and his mother. We couldn't go anywhere without my mother-in-law I.Z. He tried to give us privacy in name, but he wouldn't make a single decision without her. She was our permanent shadow, trailing behind us, between us, sometimes ahead of us, as if he needed her permission to breathe. A third wheel he had wedged into every moment, every conversation, every silence.

In truth, I was more married to her than to him.

For a long time, I thought she pulled the strings. I didn't understand then that he was completely dependent on her. Every decision in his life ran through her first. He was incapable of living a healthy, normal life without her at the center of it.

Finally, he came to me asking to sell the last piece of jewelry I owned. My wedding ring. The last thing that still meant us.

And what did he buy with the money?

Cigarettes. For his mother.

That's what my vows had been traded for. Smoke. Thin air. Ashes.

I resented him. I resented my mother-in-law I.Z. He clung to her like a lifeline while I was left collecting coins from the bottom of my bag just to buy a gallon of fuel, my palms smelling of metal and desperation.

More and more, I had to rely on my supervisor for a ride to work. The dependence had been building for weeks, one borrowed ride at a time, until I had nothing left to offer in return except honesty.

One day, worn down and starved for understanding, I let my guard slip. In a quiet moment, I admitted to my supervisor that I regretted my marriage, regretted giving in to my ex-husband before the wedding. Just a flicker of truth, a single crack in the armor I had spent years holding together.

But that small confession was twisted into an invitation. He put his hand on my knee. I removed it immediately, placing my bag between us as a barrier.

But stopping him didn't stop the consequences.

I wasn't ashamed of what he did. I was ashamed of how it might be seen, how easily the story could be rewritten, how quickly blame could be reassigned. I was ashamed that my honesty, my humanity, could become ammunition.

So, in my fear, I turned to the only woman I thought might help: my mother-in-law I.Z. I told her everything. I trusted her with the truth.

She used it as a weapon.

She and my ex-husband went behind my back, straight to my workplace. They met with the CEO. They sat across from the men who already had their version of the story, and even though the premise was that she went there to defend my honor, they both nodded and allowed them to tell their version unchallenged.

I wasn't even in the room to defend myself.

And soon after, I was fired.

We were already drowning financially, and now I had nothing. No income. No voice. No justice.

That same week, I interviewed with another company for a medical representative position. They offered me the job on the spot. To start, I needed a work permit from the labor department. My father-in-law W.S pulled a few strings to speed it up. I got the permit. I took the job.

After that, our fights became less frequent, not because anything had improved, but because I had stopped expecting anything to change. I had resigned myself to the life I had chosen, or maybe the life that had been chosen for me.

And divorce? Divorce wasn't an option. Leaving so soon after the wedding would have caused a scandal, and in our world, the woman always bore the blame. My insecurities whispered that I would never be loved again that I would end up alone. So, I stayed. I endured. And I learned to breathe underwater.

We lived in an apartment buried in the middle of nowhere, four lonely units and the landlord's house. No traffic. No buses. No phone lines. Mobile phones existed, but they were still rare, a luxury far beyond our reach.

Silence became our third companion. It filled every corner, echoing louder than any argument could.

As a dentist in the Royal Medical Services, my ex-husband was transferred to a remote military base and came home only on weekends, traveling by military transport planes.

And his absence brought peace.

Chapter 6: The First Light

I became close to our neighbor A.M, another newlywed, just as young, just as uncertain. Her husband worked long hours, so we spent our days together. She could hear my car from down the road and would start making coffee, waiting at her door before I even parked. I'd stop by her apartment before going to mine. She became my best friend. My lifeline.

A year passed. Life grew calmer, quieter, the kind of stillness that tricks you into thinking things are finally safe.

My maternal instincts were awakening, and we decided to have a baby. I became pregnant almost immediately. My ex-husband still worked at the military base during the week, coming home only on weekends. So, I carried the pregnancy and the loneliness entirely on my own.

Morning sickness? It was all-day sickness. Every smell turned against me. Every drive ended with me pulling over, nauseated, trembling. I couldn't even keep down the food I cooked myself.

My neighbor A.M would send over a plate from whatever she had made that day, and I would return the gesture when I could. We cared for each other in ways our husbands never did.

I walked a lot for work, often passing fruit stands bright with color and heavy with sweetness. I'd stand there, inhaling the scent of peaches and plums I couldn't afford. Sometimes I had just enough for a single piece. Other times, not even that.

At my parents' house, fruit had always been plentiful, three or four kinds filling the table every weekend. There was food. Comfort. Warmth. I had never known hunger until marriage. Now I was pregnant, starving emotionally and physically, and the contrast hit me like a punch to the chest.

I began to resent my ex-husband even more, not only for what he was, but for what I had lost: the softness, the safety, the sense of being cared for. My parents never stopped supporting me financially. Without them, I don't know how we would have survived. And still, I worked through every wave of nausea, through every dizzy spell, through the ache of knowing I was doing this alone.

One day, while visiting a doctor with my supervisor, he glanced at me and said, "You'd better take her home, or you'll be driving her to the hospital by the end of the day."

I was in labor.

That evening, I went to see my OB-GYN. She said I could go home for now and return to the hospital when the contractions became more intense. The next morning, we went. I was admitted and stayed in labor for more than twelve hours. I gave birth to my son, my B.S, at one a.m.

The hospital was full. His entire extended family showed up, my father-in-law W.S, his grandmother's brother and wife, aunts, uncles, cousins. Everyone came to witness the birth of the first grandchild on his mother's side.

During delivery, my doctor had to perform an episiotomy, cutting me to widen the birth canal. The pain of the sutures afterward was worse than the birth itself. But even that didn't stop his family from making cruel comments.

"Why are you walking like that? You're not the only woman who's ever given birth."

I didn't know what to say. I had just been torn open. And they wanted me to smile.

But none of it mattered. Because that was the day I met my son. My knight.

We had chosen his name together ahead of time. Or so I thought.

On the ride home from the hospital, my ex-husband casually told me he had changed our son's name. He chose a name he knew would trigger my father, since it was the name of a religious leader in the Sunni sector and my father was Shia. I was not asked. I was not included. The person who had grown inside me for nine months was given a name without my knowledge or consent.

When I asked why, he said the name had come to him in a dream.

It wasn't a dream. It was a declaration. A quiet act of cultural warfare disguised as inspiration. His way of reminding me whose world we lived in, and whose name would be erased from it first.

I loved my son B.S with every cell in my body. But that joy arrived already stained, shadowed by yet another quiet betrayal that no one else would ever see.

My mother-in-law I.Z was thrilled. She came over every day, beaming with a pride that transformed her completely. She had been waiting for this grandchild her whole life, and it showed in every gesture, every visit, every moment she spent with him.

One afternoon, while I was sleeping, she took the baby without telling me. I woke up to an empty apartment and panicked. Terror washed over me. I couldn't breathe. I needed him back.

That was the first time I felt the full force of unconditional love. The kind that seizes your chest. The kind that makes the world unlivable without your child in it.

Motherhood changed me. It changed everything.

I had to learn to ignore the passive-aggressive comments, the emotional jabs, the subtle digs. I had to numb myself one wound at a time. Because none of it mattered anymore. My son's well-being was the most important thing in the world.

When my maternity leave ended, we considered daycare, but my mother-in-law I.Z, who was a school principal, offered to take him with her to the daycare center there. She was so devoted to him, so completely present, that I didn't even bathe my own son until he was nearly a year and a half.

Six months later, my ex-husband joined the peacekeeping forces in Eritrea for a seven-month mission. We moved to an apartment closer to his family's house, within walking distance, before he left. He forbade me from visiting my own family during his absence because he didn't want his mother to be alone. It didn't matter that I was alone. It didn't matter that I hadn't seen my family in a long time. The only thing that mattered was his mother.

The only good thing he did was send some of his salary home, which gave me financial stability. So, I stayed. I focused on my baby. I kept my world small.

While he was away, his extended family, aunts, uncles, and cousins, would often visit my mother-in-law I.Z. They would gather around her table, share laughter, pass dishes, and enjoy each other's company. They would come to my house, take my son B.S to spend the day with them, but never once ask if I wanted to join them. I was invisible. And I watched it all from a distance.

My father-in-law W.S, an alcoholic, would come to my door and demand money. "It's my son's salary," he'd yell. And every time, I gave it to him. I didn't argue. I didn't push back. I had learned how to silence the noise.

I stopped waiting for kindness. I stopped expecting fairness. I started focusing on survival. I found peace in small things, the way my son B.S's fingers curled around mine, the smell of his hair, the sound of his breath as he slept.

Life began to look a little more promising. Not because it got easier, but because I had stopped needing it to be perfect.

She was doing the best she could with what she had been given. And sometimes, in the quiet moments between the pain, she found something worth holding on to.

A tiny hand curled around her finger.

A small chest rising and falling in the dark.

A reason to keep going.

Is this woman really me?

Chapter 7: Sacrificed at the Altar of Culture

Becoming a mother changed something deep within me. I began to see life through a new lens.

For starters, I hated my mother-in-law I.Z less. Our relationship evolved from quiet resentment to cautious tolerance, to friendship, and eventually… love.

My son B.S was beautiful. Fair skin, silky golden hair that shimmered in the light, and eyes that shifted from blue to a beautiful deep brown, gentle, wise beyond his months. People adored him. He made it easy to love him.

Everyone did, except his father.

To this day, I still don't understand what was wrong. My ex-husband treated our son with cold, cutting hostility, as if he expected a seven-month-old baby to behave like a disciplined adult. As soon as he walked through the door, all the laughter stopped. All the playing ceased. My baby and I would freeze, brace ourselves, walking on eggshells.

Our son B.S was permitted to be near us for fifteen minutes. Then he was sent to his room as if his mere presence was an inconvenience.

But a baby doesn't understand rules. He only knows love. He would crawl back out, searching for it. Every time he did, the yelling escalated. The tension thickened. The air grew heavier.

I didn't see it then. Or maybe I chose not to.

Was I under some kind of love spell, so desperate to hold on to the image of a family, that I sacrificed my instincts, my son's peace, his right to be safe? Was I blind to the emotional abuse he was enduring, or just too afraid to name it?

Around that time, my relationship with my mother-in-law I.Z began to shift. Now that we lived closer to her, she came over every morning. She made coffee, changed my son B.S's diapers, packed his daycare bag, and took him with her.

Watching her care for him with such quiet devotion, I began to wonder maybe she had loved her children in the same way. Maybe her son's loyalty to her wasn't blind. Maybe it was earned.

I used to say I married the poorest man of his background, not as a joke, not as poetic irony, but as a plain, painful truth. But the truth, like most things in life, was more complicated.

My ex-husband wasn't born into a poor family. His father W.S had inherited substantial wealth, a gas station and a building with six rental apartments. It could have secured their future. It could have given them stability. But my father-in-law W.S was cursed with addiction, and so, eventually, was my ex-husband. W.S had a drinking addiction, and within weeks of receiving his inheritance, he drank it all away. Every penny. Every drop of safety. He vanished into addiction and returned empty-handed.

That's how my ex-husband became part of what the extended family referred to as "the poor side." While his cousins attended private schools, traveled on vacations, and wore polished shoes, his family scraped by. My mother-in-law I.Z, a schoolteacher, carried the weight alone. She bought a modest house through her teachers' union, settled in a barely developed area, and vowed never to rely on the man who had shattered their foundation.

She had been through hell and carried it quietly.

Her husband was an alcoholic. An abuser. She endured his violence, his instability, and something even more insidious that no one in our culture dares to name: marital rape. So, did I.

In our world, that term doesn't exist. A married woman is expected to be available, always. Her consent is never a question. And if she dares to protest, he threatens, "I'll marry another. God allows me four." Divorce was shameful. Saying no was unthinkable. And so, women surrendered and survived the only way they could: by silencing themselves.

Now I could understand why her son was so devoted to her. It wasn't just love. It was survival. Obligation. Maybe even guilt. She had held everything together. She raised three sons on sheer willpower.

She once told me about a night my father-in-law W.S, drunk and raging, dragged her by the hair, along with their three boys, and threw them all out into the street. In the middle of the night. She ran to her father's house, humiliated and afraid. But instead of shelter, he turned her away and ordered her back to her husband. "So, what if he drinks," he said.

The more time I spent with my mother-in-law I.Z, the more I saw her scars, and the more I respected her. She started treating me with real kindness. For the first time, I felt like she saw me, not as a threat, but as a woman walking a path she knew all too well. I kept seeing more of her strength, more of her pain. And slowly, we grew closer.

I tried to silence the negativity in my mind, the shame, the self-doubt, and focus on the good I was giving, the effort I was making.

I didn't know then how little time we had left together.

When my ex-husband returned from serving with the peacekeeping forces in Eritrea, he was welcomed like a hero. The airport was packed. He was my mother-in-law I.Z's firstborn son, the first grandchild on her family's side, a charismatic dentist with a photographic memory who could recount stories with such vivid detail that people hung onto his every word. His return felt like a celebration that belonged to everyone except me.

My son B.S. The first great-grandchild on that side of the family, the child of their beloved firstborn — was adored before he even took his first steps. His arrival had elevated my ex-husband even further in the eyes of the family. And yet, the man they celebrated so deeply was the same man who gave his own son fifteen minutes of his presence before sending him away.

I had lost weight. I looked good. And somehow, that made my ex-husband more demanding for intimacy. Meanwhile, our son B.S was allowed to spend even less time with us, never more than thirty minutes before being sent away again.

After returning home, my ex-husband received a substantial bonus. He told me he wanted to leave the armed forces and open his own private practice. That was his dream. We discussed the logistics and how it would work, since we lived paycheck to paycheck. He'd work two jobs until the clinic took off and he had established a customer base.

As a devoted wife, I supported him with everything I had. I sold the new gold jewelry my family had given me after giving birth. I used the money my father had sent during the Eritrea deployment. Together, we gathered a couple of thousand dollars to help him open his clinic.

I walked for days through the city to find him a good location. I negotiated with medical equipment wholesalers. I found painters. I located elegant office furniture. I helped him build something from nothing.

All of us believed in him.

And with that clinic, the cycle of cheating began. A new form of abuse rose to the surface, this time draped in secrecy, manipulation, and betrayal. To him, cheating only counted if it involved a physical relationship. All the emotional destruction that came with other forms of infidelity didn't count. But only when he was the one doing it.

His first emotional affair, or what I believe it was, involved the clinic's first secretary. Let us call her Secretary Number One.

I noticed behaviors I tried to point out as unprofessional. To my shock, he blew up. He told me his clinic was sacred, therefore she was sacred too, and if he had to choose, he would always take her side. So, I stopped going there unless I absolutely had to.

Even though he was rarely home during the week, he made sure to spend more time at home on weekends. But like clockwork, every Friday night we would have a huge fight. What triggered it? I never knew, but we fought like enemies. By Sunday it was over. Until the next weekend.

That pattern repeated itself every week for months. A toxic routine we both seemed trapped in. Me clinging to scraps of peace. Him hiding truths behind a mask of normalcy.

Then one day, he landed in the hospital. That's when Secretary Number One called me, crying and shaking. She said she was sorry. She said she had caused his illness.

I froze. Her words didn't make sense.

When I asked him what she meant, he looked away before answering. Then, with a strange calmness, he told me.

She had confessed that she was in love with him. That she wanted him to leave me and marry her. But she didn't know how to make that happen, so she turned to darkness. She had gone to someone who promised to use black magic to make him hate me and destroy whatever bond we had. She put something in his coffee every Friday to make him hate being home.

As if betrayal alone wasn't enough, she had to poison the space between us with something darker. Something that lived in shadows.

Whether I believed her or not, it didn't matter. What mattered was that even then, even as he lay in a hospital bed, I was still the one carrying the shame, the burden, the broken pieces of a marriage he had already abandoned.

But that day, my mother-in-law I.Z took a stand I didn't expect. She firmly told my ex-husband that I was no longer only his wife. I was the mother of his child, her beloved grandson, and he would treat me with respect and preserve my dignity in private and in public.

He obliged.

Chapter 8: Between Devotion and Deception

When my ex-husband opened his clinic, he vanished into its walls. Between his day job in the army as a dentist and his evening hours at the clinic, I barely saw him anymore. At the time, I was still working as a medical representative for the same company my father-in-law W.S had helped me get a work permit for. But my heart was set elsewhere.

I wanted more. Something bigger. Something that would stretch me beyond the limits I knew.

Aventis, now dissolved and taken over by Sanofi Pharmaceuticals, was a French company known for its power and prestige. Number one in Europe, number six globally. I dreamed of working for them, walking into rooms with that badge on my chest. Their employees moved with elegance. They spoke to doctors with confidence and conviction. I used to watch them, not with envy, but with longing. I didn't want what they had. I wanted what they felt: self-assurance. Purpose. Pride. I wanted to feel like I mattered.

But I was Iraqi. There was a time when being an Iraqi citizen meant honor and respect, our identity admired. But after the Gulf War, that pride crumbled. Overnight, the world stopped seeing our people and started seeing our politics. My passport, once a symbol of belonging, became a burden I had to explain. And no matter how qualified I was, every interview ended the same way.

"We love your energy. We love your skills. But your nationality makes international travel difficult. It's a risk."

No matter how hard I worked, I was always almost enough.

Once I obtained Jordanian nationality, everything changed. With that one small, powerful document, doors that had once been bolted shut began to creak open. It was as if I had finally been handed a key I had spent years trying to forge. For the first time, I felt like I had a fighting chance.

I began interviewing again, this time with real hope. With each interview, I saw possibilities instead of obstacles.

And then Aventis called. I had an interview, then a second, then a third, then a fourth. Each time, I reminded my ex-husband what the job entailed: long hours, frequent travel, late-night lectures, symposiums. It also came with a significant pay increase, health insurance, and a brand-new car. I didn't want him to later say he didn't know. I didn't want miscommunication to sabotage me. I needed this dream to be mine.

Then came the fifth interview with the regional manager. I was sure this was it. Instead, he looked at me kindly and said, "We chose to go with someone else."

I held my smile like a shield. But inside, I crumbled.

Still, ambition pulsed through my veins. I had been interviewing with other prestigious pharmaceutical companies and wasn't ready to let go of my dream. A few months later, I was invited to another Aventis interview, this time on a weekend at the Dead Sea. That alone felt surreal.

Then silence. Again.

Eventually, I received an offer from a respected Saudi pharmaceutical company, scheduled to start on May twentieth, just five days before my son B. S's birthday on May fifteenth.

We were celebrating his first birthday. I had invited everyone: family, friends, and neighbors. The house overflowed with balloons, snacks, and laughter. The scent of cake drifted from the oven, warm and sweet. My heart swelled with gratitude. I was building a life, not just for me, but for him. I wanted his birthday to be perfect, a memory we could both hold onto as I stepped into something new. One foot in motherhood. One foot in ambition. And somehow, I was trying to carry both with grace.

And then the phone rang.

The screen flashed a name I hadn't expected: Sanofi/Aventis regional manager. The same man who had rejected me once. With no greeting, no small talk, he said, "Are you still interested in working with us?"

My heart skipped.

"Yes."

"Good. Bring your résumé to my office within the hour. I'm leaving the country tomorrow."

I froze. I didn't have my car or my résumé. Guests were still arriving. My hair wasn't done. My clothes weren't ironed.

But I knew exactly who to call: my mother-in-law I.Z.

The woman who had once been the source of my unhappiness had become my biggest ally, my steadfast supporter. Since this job was demanding and she was the person caring for my son B.S, I needed her blessing. She would take care of him when I worked late and when I had to travel. Without hesitation, she said, "Go. This is your moment."

I ran out the door. I caught a cab to my ex-husband's clinic, grabbed the car, and drove like the wind. But the roads near the office were closed because of a protest. I jumped out of the car and ran. Fast. Determined. I had one hour to determine my future, and I wasn't going to let it slip away.

I arrived breathless but composed. The manager looked up, smiled, and asked a single question: "When can you start?"

"Tomorrow," I said, my voice steady, my heartbeat deafening.

He smiled again and laid out the salary and benefits. Three times my current income.

I kept my face calm. But inside, I wanted to scream. Cry. Laugh. Dance. When I got home, I did all four.

I was the first married mother they had ever hired. Everyone whispered I wouldn't survive the probation period.

But I did. Not just survive. I thrived. For five years, with every presentation, every symposium, every doctor I stood before, I found pieces of myself. My confidence grew. My voice deepened with conviction. People who once overlooked me began to respect me. Some even feared me.

I was no longer the girl who begged for permission. I had become the woman people turned to for guidance.

That year, we shattered our targets. The company rewarded us with a seven-day trip to Palma de Mallorca, Spain, all expenses paid, plus spending money. Everyone celebrated.

But I couldn't. Not yet. I needed his permission.

And he said no.

His reason? "My mother is already taking care of our son while you work. We can't ask her to do more so you can go have fun."

Fun. That's what he called my victory. I wanted to scream. Didn't he see what I had become? How far had I come? This wasn't a vacation. It was a reward for my blood, my sweat, my sleepless nights.

But I didn't scream. I handed my passport to the company to get the visa and kept my silence. Deep down, I believed in fate. If it was meant to happen, it would.

And it did.

One week before the flight, my mother-in-law I.Z, my steadfast and beautiful ally, told him I should go. She reminded him of everything I had sacrificed. She defended me like I was her own daughter.

And I went.

That trip wasn't just a break. It was a window to the vast world and its potential. I stood in Spain, thousands of miles from the weight of my marriage, and felt like a woman again, full, present, free.

But even as I regained my confidence, my ex-husband still managed to pull the strings. Like a puppet master, he controlled how I spent my money, where it went, and when. The only thing he deemed worthy of my savings was his clinic. Never me. Never us.

One day, I decided it was time to buy an apartment. I was working. The bank would give me a loan. It made sense. I brought up the idea and he agreed, with one condition: the monthly payment couldn't exceed our rent, or only slightly more.

I dreamed of something beautiful. But every decent apartment felt out of reach. So, I did what I do best. I researched. I knocked on doors. I scanned every listing in our area until I stumbled upon a new development not far from where we lived. Two small bedrooms, one and a half bathrooms, a compact living room. The first-floor unit had a patio and a parking space. Just eight hundred and sixty square feet. The payment was slightly higher than rent. It wasn't my dream home. It wasn't the kind of place my family would boast about. But it would be mine.

When I told my father, he didn't hesitate. "I'll cover the down payment," he said, and a few days later the money was in my account.

And once again, my ex-husband manipulated me.

He suggested I give him the money for "safekeeping." He said it would help him secure checks from his business account. He made it sound so simple, so logical, and just like someone in a trance, I handed it over without question. After all, the apartment was still under construction. I didn't need the money just yet.

But when the apartment was ready and the loan was approved, I asked him for the money. That's when the truth revealed itself.

"It's gone," he said flatly. "I spent it. On you."

As if I wasn't the one working a job that paid three times more than his. As if I hadn't already been carrying us both. He spent it and didn't even pretend he'd try to return it.

I felt sick. But I couldn't tell my father. I had spent years painting this man as good, decent, and honorable. I didn't want to face the truth that I had made a terrible choice. I had chosen him. I had defended him. I had believed in him.

So, I did what I always did. I fixed it. I took out a personal loan to cover the down payment.

We were almost ready to sign the mortgage papers when my mother-in-law I.Z invited me for breakfast. Even though we were on good terms and spending a great deal of time together, her priority remained constant: her son and what was best for him.

Over tea and warm bread, she looked at me gently and said, "It would be humiliating for a man to live in a house owned solely by his wife. It will create a wedge in your marriage. He will never feel like it's his home."

What she didn't say, what she didn't have to say, was the double standard sitting silently in the room between us. It hadn't been humiliating for her husband to live in a house she owned. But for me, the woman paying for everything? My ownership was a threat. No matter how much she loved me, her son's pride came first. Always.

Out of love and respect for her, I agreed. To this day, my family doesn't know he was a co-owner.

Still, I was excited. It wasn't the dream apartment, but it was ours: modest, new, full of hope.

In our culture, it's customary to deep-clean a new home, even if it's been freshly scrubbed by the builder. My mother-in-law I.Z and I planned to go together that weekend to do just that. Friday morning, before the sun rose, I got dressed and drove to her house, excited. This was our plan, our shared moment.

But my father-in-law W.S answered the door. "She's not here," he said. "She left before sunrise."

I assumed she'd gone to visit a sister and forgotten our plans. So, I drove to the apartment and asked the building supervisor for the keys.

He blinked. "A woman already came this morning and picked them up."

Confused, I went to the apartment, and there she was: soaked in water, hair tied back, sleeves rolled up, smiling like she had just won the lottery.

"I wanted to surprise you," she said.

And she did.

It was the sweetest surprise. A rare moment of pure kindness, unexpected, unprompted, unforgettable. That little gesture stayed with me for years.

We had a good life in that apartment, for a while. The warmth between my mother-in-law I.Z and me softened everything. I think even my ex-husband noticed. Maybe he began to see me again, not just as the woman carrying his world, but as someone who could truly love.

It was a brief season of peace.

Fragile. Fleeting.

Chapter 9: The Woman in the Red Robe

My mother-in-law I.Z, once so vibrant, started to complain of headaches, fatigue, drowsiness, and a strange weakness in her arms. My ex-husband took her for tests, blood work, scans, and exams. Everything came back normal. The doctor shrugged and said, "She's just seeking attention."

But then came the day that would change everything.

It was spring vacation. She was having lunch at her sister's house, and I happened to be working in that area. She called and invited me to join them on my lunch break. I did. We laughed. We ate. We drank coffee. It was light. Easy. Normal. I hugged her goodbye and returned to work, never imagining it would be the last time things felt that way.

Because nothing was normal after that day.

A phone call came, and my heart dropped before I even answered. My mother-in-law I.Z had suffered a seizure while driving home. My son B.S was in the passenger seat. She lost control of the car. My son B.S was safe, thank God, taken in by relatives who happened to be nearby. But she was in critical condition.

I dropped everything and ran to the hospital, which was overflowing. She was deeply loved and respected. People poured in, family, friends, coworkers, all with the same look: fear thinly veiled behind hope.

A doctor approached me and my ex-husband. He looked directly at us and lowered his voice. "I know you're both in the medical field," he said gently. "So, you'll understand..."

Those five words are always the beginning of heartbreak.

"She has a brain tumor," he said quietly. "It's in the speech and motor region. The swelling is what caused the seizure."

She couldn't speak clearly. Her words spilled out in fragments, disjointed and slurred. You could see it in her eyes: the panic, the humiliation, the anger at her own body for betraying her.

She was admitted for more testing, but there were no private rooms available. We sat in a crowded, noisy space while she lay there, confused and exposed. Everything had changed in a heartbeat. And yet, the world outside kept turning, oblivious to how one family's axis had just shattered.

Her family, well-connected within the military, pulled every string they could. They called in favors, reaching out to relatives with high ranks. But nothing worked. They couldn't get her into a private room.

I worked with the daughter of the director of military medical services. I reached out to her and asked for help. And what none of their powerful connections could do, I did. My mother-in-law I.Z was moved into a room reserved for VIP patients.

A few days later, the swelling began to subside. Her speech returned.

She looked so much older than her forty-six years, her once-strong frame now frail, every line on her face deepened by pain. But she smiled.

Wrapped in her red robe, she looked at me and said softly, "I prayed to God to keep me alive long enough to see my children grow up. They have. But now… I want more. More time with them."

I had never felt heartbreak like that moment. It was as if time itself paused and grieved with us.

The diagnosis was brutal: Glioblastoma Multiforme. One of the most aggressive and unforgiving brain tumors known to medicine. No cure. No surgery. Only radiation to reduce the swelling, to slow its cruel march, to borrow time.

We clung to hope. We sought second, third, and fourth opinions. But the answer was always the same: inoperable. Any attempt to remove it would leave her permanently incapacitated, if not worse. She had two to ten months to live.

For the first two months, we didn't leave her side. Her three sons took turns sleeping on the floor, curled on couches, cradled by exhaustion. I stepped in to manage everything else, cleaning, cooking, holding the household together.

And as the weight grew heavier, my ex-husband began to disappear.

At first, it was subtle. He began working late. Then came the missed calls. Then nights without contact. Until one day I realized he had withdrawn completely. Into alcohol. Into absence. Into silence.

I became the one taking her to every doctor's appointment. I sat beside her through every radiation session. She was no longer just my mother-in-law. She was my second mother. And I was her daughter, by choice, not by blood.

Somewhere in the chaos of caregiving and working full-time, I discovered I was pregnant.

I was carrying life while watching death inch closer every day. I was nurturing two people at once: one growing inside me, and one slowly slipping away.

And all the while, I had a suspicion my ex-husband was cheating on me. I saw the signs. I felt them. But I chose to ignore them. I told myself maybe this new relationship was helping him cope. Maybe if someone else could soothe his pain, it would help him survive this heartbreak. I knew that the possibility of losing his mother would break him, and I convinced myself I wasn't enough to hold him together alone.

I swallowed my pride and told myself it was love. That it was sacrifice.

My ex-husband had a very clever way of lying without technically lying. I called them half-truths. He wore honesty like a badge of honor, always reminding me how truthful he was, while he lied by omission. He'd say things like, "A colleague and I talked about this book, you'll love it. She sent it to you." Or "A friend brought me food and she wanted you to try it, so she sent you some." He would ask, "Does it bother you that I have a female friend? Because if it does, I will stop being friends with her." He made concern sound like confession. He made manipulation sound like consideration.

Then all the signs began to line up. The phone was glued to him at all times, even in the bathroom. Phone calls on the balcony that stretched into hours. Even during a weekend getaway, I had booked for us, he'd disappear. "One quick call," he'd say. Then he'd be gone for the rest of the evening.

I kept pretending not to care. Not to feel the shift. Not to notice how I was becoming irrelevant. Until he stopped pretending too. The brazenness grew. He didn't care if I noticed anymore. My feelings became an afterthought, if they were ever a thought at all.

And while he enjoyed playing the role of Romeo, I took his place in caring for his mother.

One night, I couldn't sleep. Pregnancy had made every position uncomfortable. I tossed and turned, hoping exhaustion would win, when suddenly his phone lit up beside me. A message flashed across the screen: vacation plans with that female friend and colleague.

Something inside me snapped. Not in rage, but in icy clarity.

I sat up. Picked up the phone. Called her. I calmly introduced myself and told her simply: "If you want to take my place, take it. Fill my shoes. I'll step aside and give it all up. You can have him, with everything that comes with him. I'd rather be divorced than live as a fool."

I went back home and told my ex-husband exactly what I'd done. I gave him until the end of the day to decide me or her.

Eventually, he came home, tears streaming down his face, dropping to his knees, begging like a man facing execution. He swore he couldn't live without me. He said he was relieved I had called her. He painted her as a predator, a woman who had preyed on his grief and loneliness.

"She trapped me," he said. "I was only playing along. She used my sadness over my mother to pull me in."

And I, gullible, exhausted, pregnant, desperate for stability, for some sliver of peace, believed him.

Now, looking back, I see how masterfully he spun his lies. How he wove guilt and grief into a blanket of deception and tucked me tightly under it.

Through it all, my mother-in-law I.Z was the source of strength and hope for all of us. She would hum softly, over and over: *"Life is beautiful… if only we understood it."*

She loved me. Not just tolerated but loved me. Not like a daughter-in-law, but like a daughter she never had.

When I had to travel for a three-day work trip, even though she was immunocompromised, even though every doctor warned her not to risk it, she insisted on coming to the airport. She stood there, wrapped in layers against the chill, hugged me tight, and whispered through her tears: "These were the longest three days of my life. If they'd let me, I'd wait for you right at the gate."

She couldn't wait for me to come home.

But not all goodbyes come with warning.

She kept moving. Cooking. Folding laundry. Clinging to routine like it was the only thread holding her to life. She refused to surrender until the tumor forced her to.

Then her body began to betray her. She could no longer shift positions on her own. Even turning in bed became impossible. My son B.S was still spending all his time with her, his presence a small joy in the thick fog of her pain. But caring for a toddler had become too much. Before the experience could turn into trauma for either of them, we enrolled him in preschool.

We stopped going home. Our lives circled around her now.

Her own mother was still alive, but every visit left her shattered, so much so that she collapsed into grief and had to be admitted to the ICU. Her sisters, burdened with caring for their own mother, offered little help. So, it was me and my ex-husband's two younger brothers, three of us shouldering the slow, suffocating weight of watching her fade away.

And just as the doctor had predicted, as if death kept a calendar hidden in its coat pocket, my mother-in-law I.Z passed away at the ten-month mark.

The funeral was full. She was loved. Respected. Cherished.

And yet, the man she loved most, her firstborn, was so drunk, so medicated, he could barely stand. He was drooling, incoherent, making a spectacle of himself in front of everyone who had come to honor her.

People pulled me aside and begged, "Please, keep him inside. We're all grieving, and he's humiliating the family."

And I did. Because even then, I protected him. Even at her funeral. Even when she was the one who deserved protection.

But before my mother-in-law I.Z slipped away, she looked into my eyes, once fierce, now glassy with pain, and said, "Take care of my family."

And I did.

For years, I carried them all on my back, her sons, her sisters, her entire family. I wanted to be the one who honored her legacy, who kept the promise I had made at her deathbed, because I had made it not out of obligation but out of love.

Because I loved her. Because someone had to.

As for my ex-husband, he spent two years after her death drunk, a shell of a human, using language I never knew existed. Two years of covering for him and trying to keep his image intact to the outside world.

I don't know how to define the woman I was at that point.

Who was she? Where did she begin, and where did she vanish?

Was that woman really me?

Chapter 10: The Beast Unleashed

I don't know if my ex-husband had always been mentally unstable and my mother-in-law I.Z had been the force that kept him grounded. Because after her death, something in him shifted, subtly at first, then rapidly and without apology. From that moment on, nothing felt sacred anymore.

Two months after we buried her, on January first, I gave birth to my daughter N.K.S. A new life arriving in the shadow of loss. Suddenly, I was a mother for the second time, grieving and healing, yet already preparing to return to work. And somehow, in the middle of it all, I had become responsible for holding the entire family together.

I had to hire help to care for the children while I worked and to manage the cooking for a large family every day. Still, the weight of it all became too much. My son B.S was struggling emotionally after losing his grandmother, and my job demanded long hours and constant focus.

Almost a year after her death, I left the job I loved most. Not because I didn't love it anymore, and not because it was exhausting, but because I wanted to be there for my children. I worked because I loved my career and we needed the money, but each day I carried the guilt of leaving them for so many hours.

So, when my ex-husband said his clinic was thriving and that he could provide for us, I believed him. Not out of naivety, but out of hope. I wanted it to be true.

Three months later, the illusion shattered. The bills piled up, the mortgage fell behind, the help was gone, and we were drowning in debt. We were borrowing money to buy groceries just to feed his family, while he kept insisting everything was under control. By the end of that third month, we had no choice but to put our apartment up for sale. And I had to go back to work, only this time I had lost the job I loved and had to accept a lower-paying, less fulfilling position just to keep us afloat.

Eventually, we sold our apartment. The home I had worked for, the mortgage I had carried, the security I had tried to build for our family, it all came down to that. Even though he hadn't contributed a single dinar toward the purchase or the payments, he was still legally entitled to half the sale. And he took it without hesitation, without shame, without a moment of recognition for everything I had sacrificed to keep us afloat.

My father had purchased an investment property just down the road from ours, a larger apartment in a better location. After some time and many difficult conversations, my parents agreed to let us live there once the tenants' lease ended, for free. We only had to pay the bills and annual taxes.

It took a full year before the tenants finally moved out, and when they did, they left the place in shambles. It was my responsibility to restore it out of my share from the apartment sale. After all, he was not going to invest in a property that didn't belong to him.

My father, seeing the chaos from a distance, made it clear: this apartment would be mine. But he refused to put the deed in my name. He knew the kind of man my ex-husband was. He knew that if the apartment were under my name, my ex-husband would pressure me to sell it, and I would cave. He knew I'd end up homeless, discarded, with no remorse from the man I was sacrificing everything for.

He was right. One billion percent right.

For more than six years, my father-in-law W.S, my brothers-in-law S.S, and their wives came to dinner every single day without exception. His aunts from his mother's side joined us every weekend. Just like that, our home became the family house.

Looking back now, I wonder if my devotion had less to do with the promise I had made to I.Z and more to do with an ache I didn't yet understand, an unconscious need to surround myself with others, to keep the house full so I wouldn't have to face the emptiness of being alone with him.

I'm not complaining. In fact, that may have been the best period in our relationship. It brought out something in me, something nurturing, strong, generous. It revealed the kind of woman I truly was.

But I will never forget the night my daughter T.K.S was born, in September 2007. She was barely hours old. I had just been through labor, my body exhausted, my heart full, when my ex-husband suggested we go grocery shopping. Not tomorrow. Not in a few days. The next morning, less than twenty-four hours after giving birth, I was in a supermarket pushing a cart, buying food to cook iftar for his brothers S.S and his father W.S and their wives.

They were all married by then. They had wives of their own. And still, it fell to me.

I didn't say a word. I never did. But something inside me, already stretched so thin, quietly noted the moment and filed it away.

There were nights when he stormed out of the house with nothing but rage carrying him forward, disappearing into the darkness while I stood frozen between fear and hope. Hope that he will come back alive. Fear of the version of him that might walk back through the door. Sometimes he returned hours later, drunk, unsteady, full of accusations that made no sense. Other nights I chased him barefoot into the street, trying to shield him from himself, trying to shield the world from seeing what we had become.

There were nights he ran out completely naked, and I ran after him, begging him to come back before anyone saw. Almost every night, he wet the bed, and I would quietly clean it up before dawn, inventing excuses to protect his dignity and what was left of mine.

As if that wasn't enough, I had to take the fall for everything he failed to do at work. No matter how many alarms I set, no matter how many times I shook him awake or called his phone, he wouldn't get up. His general from the military hospital would call me directly, demanding to know why he hadn't shown up. I became the buffer between him and the world, the one who answered for him, explained for him, covered for him.

And he used me as his scapegoat.

He told his general that I had taken his keys and his phone by mistake, that he had been trapped inside the house and couldn't leave. That was the story he gave them. That was the version of reality they chose to hear.

And I let it stand.

I let them believe I was the irresponsible one. I let myself become the joke, the one whispered about, mocked in the hallways. Because somehow, protecting him felt easier than facing the truth: that I was disappearing. That I was being erased inside the life I was fighting so hard to hold together.

Near the end of those two years, his grandmother passed away. Her death stirred new tension. He and his siblings didn't receive their mother's share of the inheritance, but some aunts and uncles gave them a few thousand each. That money helped my brothers-in-law S.S get engaged. My ex-husband used his share to upgrade his car.

Toward the end of that second year, we took a short weekend getaway with one of his aunts and her daughters, and his youngest brother. It was a four-hour drive. As soon as we checked in, he wanted to go out. I knew exactly what that meant: alcohol. I begged him not to. "Please," I said, "let's just enjoy this weekend, go to the beach, be with family." But he left anyway.

Drunk and reckless, he totaled his brand-new car. We had to return home in a taxi, paying hundreds of dollars for the ride. He was furious at the cost, at the consequences, but mostly at his aunt for refusing to lend him money to fix the car. He called her names and I will not repeat. I was horrified.

Later, he admitted that what upset him most was that he didn't even get a scratch from the accident. He had wanted something visible, anything to show for the mess he was in.

Ironically, just two days after the car came back from the repair shop, he crashed again. This time, he slammed his head into the windshield. The deep gash left a permanent scar on his forehead, exactly where he had once pointed and wished for a mark.

That, somehow, was his wake-up call.

He finally stopped drinking.

Chapter 11: The Righteous Abuser

My ex-husband never lived a balanced life. Everything about him was extreme.

When he worked, he was consumed by it entirely. When he drank, he was never just tipsy and never truly sober. When he turned to drugs, there was no ceiling to what he would consume. And when he turned to religion, it was not gentle or grounding. It was absolute.

After two years of indulgence and destruction, he declared it was time to repent. And I was drafted into his redemption.

Suddenly, music was forbidden. The television stayed off whenever he was home. I had to memorize a page of the Quran every single day. I was expected to wake him up at dawn to pray and to pray alongside him, whether I felt connected or not. My faith, my relationship with God, my spiritual life, none of it belonged to me anymore. It belonged to his performance of righteousness.

By then we had three children: my son B.S, my daughter N.K.S, and my youngest T.K.S. He had left the army and was working full-time in his clinic. Patients were beginning to trust him, and more of them came every day. We were living in a rent-free apartment, which meant I could finally step back from work and focus on raising our children without the constant pressure of survival.

Life was peaceful. More than peaceful, it almost felt charmed. He treated me like a goddess, as if no other woman existed on earth. As if I were the last woman left after an apocalypse, and he was the luckiest survivor simply because he had me.

And I believed it.

I believed the warmth, the attention, the admiration. I believed the version of love where I was lifted so high that I could no longer see the ground beneath me. For a time, it felt like everything I had endured had been worth it. That maybe love could redeem the years that had nearly broken me.

But like I said before, his abuse followed a cycle. Five years of calm before the storm. Five years of peace, five years of affection, five years of believing we had finally arrived somewhere safe, before the world shattered again.

Secretary Number Two was kind. She treated me with respect and dignity. She saw me as a wife, a mother, a woman, not a threat. But when she got married and left the clinic, he needed to hire someone new. That's when Secretary Number Three entered our lives.

This time, I didn't see the betrayal coming.

We were in what I believed was the best place we had ever been. Our children were stable, the clinic was thriving, we were laughing again. I had allowed myself to exhale, just a little.

Then one morning, he looked at me with such devotion that I almost melted. He said, "If I had a choice, I would ask to be your husband in heaven. You would be the only woman in my paradise."

And I believed him.

By that same evening, he told me he was going to marry a second wife.

To go from *"you are the only woman in my eternity"* to *"I am taking another wife"* in less than twelve hours feels like being lifted to the clouds only to be dropped without warning. No parachute. No ground beneath you. Just freefall.

He knew exactly how to elevate me. And he knew exactly how to destroy me.

When I questioned his reasons, the most absurd words came tumbling out of his mouth. He said he wanted to go to Afghanistan to join jihad, and that he needed another wife to accompany him. He said he loved me and our children too much to take us with him, as if that were an act of mercy rather than an insult.

I stared at him and said, "Then you must divorce me first."

I would not allow my name or my children's names to be tied to a criminal. I had always been fiercely against violence in all forms. Religion, honor, patriotism, none of those labels could disguise murder or fanaticism. That was a line I would never cross.

And that was the moment something shifted.

From then on, he launched a psychological war, one that twisted truth and bent reality. He made himself the martyr, the misunderstood hero, the man with a divine calling. He painted me as weak, faithless, ungrateful. He weaponized religion, culture, guilt, and motherhood, every vulnerability he knew I carried.

What followed wasn't loud. It wasn't physical. It was slow. Deliberate. Erosive. A dismantling of self, one whispered humiliation at a time.

He began planting seeds, small at first, half-truths dressed as confessions, stories designed to make me doubt my own reality.

The first was about Secretary Number Three. He painted her as a savior. According to him, she was the one who had stopped him from divorcing me. He said she begged him not to abandon the mother of his children. He spoke of her as if she understood our love better than I did. And then, as a gesture of gratitude, he invited her into our home.

Every instinct in my body tightened. But I swallowed my discomfort. I told myself to be gracious, to be composed, to be the bigger person. I had done that all my life, made myself smaller to make others comfortable. So, I opened the door and let her step inside.

Not realizing I was welcoming the beginning of my own replacement.

Soon after, he mentioned casually that he often drove her home at night because they worked late. Sometimes until midnight. He said it like it was nothing, but the way he paused and looked at me said everything. He was waiting to see if I would break.

And like the version of myself he had spent years sculpting, I smiled and said, "I don't mind. I trust you."

But something cracked. Not loudly. Quietly. A hairline fracture across the foundation of who I thought we were.

Then the story changed again. Suddenly he no longer wanted to go to Afghanistan. He said my words had resonated with him. He said he had reconsidered because of my wisdom, my strength, my love. It sounded like repentance. But it was simply the next act in a script he was writing without me.

Because now there was a new problem. He said he had to marry her, not because he loved her, he emphasized, but because he had already made her a promise. And he was not the kind of man who went back on his word.

This was the same man who lied to his commanding general, who lied to his patients, who lied to me for years. But suddenly honor mattered, when it came to another woman. It was almost poetic in its cruelty.

What followed was a masterful web of lies, distortions, and gaslighting, story layered upon story, fiction upon fiction, until eventually he admitted the truth, or rather a carefully edited version of it. Secretary Number Three was not simply a colleague. She was the mysterious woman he had planned to take to Afghanistan. He had invited her into our home not out of gratitude but because he was already imagining a future with her woven into the fabric of our life. He wasn't just thinking about marrying her. He was considering bringing her to live with us. In my parents' apartment. The home that was supposed to be my refuge.

And he said all of this with the tone of someone offering me a gift.

"You can go back to work," he told me, his voice warm and persuasive. "Pursue your ambitions. She will stay home with the children. She'll do the housework. We'll be one big happy family. You two could be best friends."

He said it with a smile. As if he were proposing generosity. As if tearing apart the home I had built was an act of love.

I refused. I told him plainly: he had to choose. There would be no shared husband, no two-wives-under-one-roof arrangement. I would not raise my children in a home where I had to shrink myself to make space for the woman replacing me.

Eventually, he said he would choose me. But that was never the end of it. Because it was never the end of it.

She still worked with him until midnight. He still picked her up every morning and dropped her off every night. Life continued as if my refusal had been nothing more than a momentary inconvenience, something to be waited out, not respected.

One day, he came home with his clothes torn, chest heaving with theatrical indignation. He stood in the doorway like a martyr returning from battle and launched into a dramatic story about how her neighbor had confronted him, a man supposedly interested in proposing to her. According to him, the confrontation escalated into a full fight, not just with the neighbor but with two other men, including the man's elderly father. He described how he fought them all. How strong he was. How he overpowered them.

He even bragged that he pushed the old man so hard he fell backward into the street.

He told it with pride.

As if violence were something to admire. As if harming an elderly man made him powerful. I stood there in silence, disgusted. But then he became enraged that I didn't admire him. He yelled about how ungrateful I was, how blessed I should feel to be married to someone like him. He wanted praise. He wanted worship.

Then, within a week, news came that the neighbor's father had died.

He felt no remorse. Not a flicker of regret. Not even a pause. This man who had once shaken me awake for dawn prayer and demanded I recite Quran by heart had no reaction to the possibility that his violence had contributed to another human being's death.

Nothing. Just pride in his strength.

Sometime during that period, I found myself in his clinic with all three children. My youngest T.K.S was barely a year old, asleep in my arms, her tiny head resting on my shoulder as I sat in his office waiting for him to finish with a patient. I had imagined a quiet wait. A moment of stillness. Maybe even a breath.

I was wrong.

Secretary Number Three walked in and sat on the table just inches from me, close enough that I could feel her breath. She looked me directly in the eyes, steady and unblinking, and spoke with a coldness that didn't need to be loud to cut.

"I love your husband and I want to marry him," she said. "Our religion allows four wives, and you're the only one standing in the way. I'm willing to live with him in one room with nothing but a rug on the floor. Haven't you had enough of him? You've had him for twelve years. Isn't that enough?"

I froze. My body went cold. Tears slipped down my cheeks before I even realized I was crying.

Before I could speak, my ex-husband walked into the room. I told him right there, in front of her, exactly what she had said.

He smirked.

"I don't mind having two women fighting for me," he said, as if our lives were entertainment, as if my heartbreak were nothing but a game.

I could have screamed. I could have shattered the room, exposed them both in front of every patient sitting just outside the door. But I didn't. I thought about his reputation as a doctor. About the clinic he had worked so hard to build. Even in the moment I was being humiliated, even as my heart broke in front of the woman who wanted to replace me, I protected him.

Because I was still the one who understood what it meant to lose everything.

I walked out of that clinic with my baby T.K.S in my arms, my daughters N.K.S trailing beside me, and a silence inside me that felt like it could swallow the world. My hands were shaking. My chest felt hollow.

I wasn't working. He was the sole provider. My children depended on him. If I exploded, if I burned the moment down to ashes, I could lose everything. And he knew it.

But I couldn't stay silent. Silence would have meant surrender.

So, I called her father. My voice was unsteady but clear. I told him exactly what his daughter had said to me. Every word. Every insult. Every intention. I hoped, naively, that he would be shocked. That he might put an end to it.

Instead, he was thrilled.

"It would be a blessing," he said, "if your husband married my daughter."

As if I were a formality. As if my marriage was already over.

Half an hour later, my phone rang. It was my ex-husband. Raging. He screamed that I had ruined everything. He swore that if I didn't go to their house and apologize in person within thirty minutes, I would face consequences I didn't want to imagine.

Driven by terror, I took two Xanax, lifted myself off the floor, and went.

I stepped over every shred of dignity I had left and offered an apology to the very people who had orchestrated my humiliation. And my ex-husband was there to witness it in person. He stood to the side, arms crossed, watching. Not intervening. Not defending. Not even flinching. He watched the mother of his children bow her head and apologize to the woman who wanted to take her place.

And he felt nothing. Not guilt. Not conflict. Not shame.

Only victory.

That apology emboldened her. She began texting me directly, targeting my deepest insecurities with precision, as if he had handed her a map of my most vulnerable places. For the first time in my life, I found myself writing words meant to wound. Not just defensive. Cutting. And while I kept my composure on the outside, each exchange left bruises on my soul.

It wasn't who I was. I had always been someone who cared too deeply about how my words landed. But now I was trying to hurt someone. And it hurt me too.

Everyone around us knew. The affair was no longer a secret. Neighbors stopped going to the clinic. People offered looks of sympathy but never action. Never a stand.

And yet I had them all over for dinner almost every night. Feeding the mouths that refused to speak up. Hosting the silence that kept me caged.

That silence stayed exactly the same until the day I left the country and left their brother behind.

I lost thirty-five pounds. My body bore the weight of everything my voice couldn't say. I went from a size sixteen to a size two. My face hollowed. My eyes lost their light. People began asking if I had cancer. But no one could see that the sickness wasn't in my body. It was in my home.

And just like that, the narrative changed again. He swore she meant nothing. He'd do anything to win me back. And so, the cycle reset. The old familiar honeymoon phase returned. Flowers. Promises. Empty eyes rehearsing apologies.

Around that time, a door quietly opened.

An old family friend, one of my parents' long-time acquaintances who owned a private school, had always admired me for my intelligence and upbringing. When we reconnected, she didn't hesitate. She offered me a teaching position: science and math from first through eighth grade, and science in Arabic for fourth through sixth. The pay was modest compared to what I had earned as a pharmacist, but the opportunity was priceless.

The school ran from preschool through high school, and my children could attend with me. I received a significant discount on their tuition and had paid summer vacations. It was perfect. We would go to school together and come home together. I could watch over them, know their friends, and make sure they were surrounded by children from families with good values.

I stayed there for five years. And those years became one of the most unexpectedly joyful periods of my life.

For the first time, I worked in an environment made up mostly of women. I made real friendships, the kind where I could tell jokes, laugh freely, and sip coffee without calculating every word or glance.

My previous jobs had been male-dominated environments where professionalism was armor, and every smile was a calculation. I had learned not to show cracks, not to open up, not to bring marital pain into rooms where men could use it, twist it, or pity it. Vulnerability was a luxury I couldn't afford.

But here, in this new space, I could finally breathe.

Every morning, I brought breakfast for the teachers. I couldn't eat while people watched, so I brought enough for everyone to share. It was my small way of creating warmth, an invitation into community without having to explain myself. Eventually, the owner gently asked me to stop, explaining it wasn't typically done. But I didn't mind.

For the first time in a long time, I felt seen. I felt normal.

Many of the women I worked with weren't there out of financial necessity. Their husbands worked for the royal family. They lived comfortably. They weren't working to survive. They were working for fulfillment, for purpose, for a sense of self beyond wife and mother.

And that inspired me. They showed me a world where a woman could exist outside of service and sacrifice. Where her identity didn't have to be tied to her husband's moods, desires, or decisions. Where she could choose who she was.

And slowly, I began to wonder who I might become if I allowed myself to exist too.

Teaching is hard. People envy teachers for the short hours and long holidays, but few understand the hours of planning, grading, and preparation that happen long after the school day ends. In that first year, I carried nineteen different curriculums and twenty-one classes to grade. The deadlines were relentless. I worked late into the evenings just to keep up.

But oddly, I didn't feel drained.

Because during this time, the clinic was thriving and my ex-husband was almost never home. And for once, that absence didn't bring anxiety. It brought peace. I could focus on my children, on my work, on my own quiet existence. I was building a life, however modest, that was mine.

And to be fair, my ex-husband was a highly skilled dentist, talented, meticulous, and gifted with his hands. His work spoke for itself and his patients adored him.

And so, again, a new honeymoon phase began. Suddenly he was gentle. Attentive. Devoted. He showered me with compliments, told me how beautiful I was, how lucky he felt to have me, how he couldn't imagine life without me.

And it was intoxicating. Because after surviving starvation, even crumbs feel like a feast. After pain, even counterfeit tenderness can feel like love.

Chapter 12: Secretary Number Four

And then came E.D.

She was married and a mother, from a modest background. Because of that, I assumed she wasn't a threat. I told myself she wasn't after him. She carried herself with confidence and with a kind of stubbornness that didn't bend easily.

He complained about her constantly. He called her a snob, said she didn't listen, that she did things her own way.

But now I understand.

She wasn't a snob. She wasn't disrespectful. She was simply a woman he couldn't control. She wasn't broken. She challenged him. And he set his mind on breaking her. He said it openly, in those exact words, whenever he complained about her. He wanted to tame her.

She had boundaries. She had a sense of self. She was not shaped by fear or the need to please. She didn't flinch when he raised his voice. She didn't shrink to make room for him. And to a man like him, a woman who could not be controlled was not just unacceptable. She was a puzzle he needed to conquer.

Even though she wasn't beautiful by traditional standards, and she wasn't highly educated, and she didn't come from a powerful family, she carried herself with a confidence that took up space. She was full of herself in a way I didn't know how to be.

She had something I lacked then: self-worth. Self-respect. Self-confidence.

And she knew about the events with Secretary Number Three. She knew what had happened. So instead of competing with me, she stood beside me. She told me she had my back. She became my cheerleader, not because she wanted something from me, but because she did not fear him.

She wasn't impressed by him. She didn't shrink in his presence. She didn't perform for approval. She existed in her own skin comfortably, and I watched her and realized, painfully, that I did not.

But eventually, he would find a way to break her and, in the process, break everything else. Because that is what men like him do. When they cannot control a woman, they don't simply walk away. They dismantle her piece by piece and destroy anything standing in the way of that conquest.

And while he was busy trying to tame E.D, he was also undoing the fragile peace I had built, the stability I was finally beginning to taste. His obsession with conquering her would become the wrecking ball that shattered the life I had spent years holding together with my bare hands.

Once again, we fell back into the same old pattern, the doctor and secretary cycle. A rhythm I knew too well:

He elevates → She admires → I trust → He betrays → I break → He repents → We heal → A new secretary enters → and the cycle begins again.

It was never about love. It was never about companionship. It was about power. A rotating stage of women, each one chosen for a different purpose: one to worship him, one to challenge him, one to fill the silence, one to remind him he was desired.

And I? I was the constant. The anchor. The home. The woman who stayed. The one he returned to when his world fell apart, so he could begin the cycle all over again.

His reputation had reached new heights. Appointments were booked three months in advance, and patients crowded the stairway waiting for a chance to be seen. The success was undeniable, and it was time to expand.

And as always, I stepped in.

With everything I had saved and everything I could access through my family, I helped him grow the business. He took over the entire floor of the building where his clinic was located. Now he had four dental units and a panoramic X-ray machine to serve orthodontic patients who needed braces. It was a proud moment for him. For the clinic. For the image we projected to the world.

But behind that success was a familiar truth: I was the silent architect behind the curtain, investing in his future while still trying to salvage my own.

His talent was undeniable. He was a magician in the world of dentistry, especially with surgical procedures. Word began to spread far beyond our city. Patients were calling from the United States, Austria, and the Gulf, Qatar, the UAE, planning their vacations around their appointments with him. He had mastered dental implants, produced flawless veneers, and added Botox and fillers to his list of services.

And just like that, the money started pouring in.

But with success came chaos. He had no interest in the responsibility that came with financial growth. Bills were forgotten; accounts were left unmonitored. So, he handed full control to E.D, now promoted to office manager. He brought on two more dentists to work under his supervision.

The hunger grew. Money. Fame. Power. Twelve-hour days turned into sixteen. It still wasn't enough.

So, he turned to drugs.

It started quietly, something to give him a boost, to stay awake, to keep going. But it didn't stop. The drugs became the fuel he relied on to function. I tried to talk him out of it, begging him to slow down. I told him it was unsustainable, that it would destroy him.

But he was already hooked.

And then he started offering it to me. I said no. I said it clearly. But saying no was never enough with him. When I refused, he forced it on me. He would shove the pills into my mouth and cover my mouth and nose with his hand so I couldn't spit them out. He did it with the same calmness someone might use to close a door. No panic. No rage. Just certainty in his ownership over my body.

And that was when I realized: this wasn't about drugs. It was about control. Again. Total, merciless control.

One day while I was at work, my phone rang. It was him, his voice eerily calm. He told me he had been arrested for drug use and needed me to call one of his relatives to bail him out. Then, almost as an afterthought, he instructed me to tell everyone he was away attending a conference.

As if it were nothing. As if this were just another inconvenience. As if I were still responsible for maintaining the myth of who he pretended to be.

And I did. I followed his script. I protected his image. I played the loyal wife, even as my world tilted under me.

It took a few days before he was released. During that time, I held my breath, lied through my teeth, and juggled the weight of a secret that wasn't mine to carry. After his release, he swore, like so many times before, that he would never do it again. He told me the charges had been dropped but warned that if there was ever a next time, he could be prosecuted for possession with intent to distribute.

I let out a long, weary sigh of relief. Not because I believed him, but because for the moment, I needed to believe in the pause.

And for a while, it seemed like he kept his promise. He stopped using or at least hid it well enough to convince me. Our life settled into something resembling structure. He started coming home before the kids went to sleep. He'd let them into the room for a few minutes before dismissing them and demanding silence. I hated that. I hated the way he rationed his affection like it was currency. But compared to what we had lived through, it felt like a blessing. A distorted version of peace.

But peace, nonetheless.

He was never a man of moderation. As his reputation grew, he became even more consumed by work. The fleeting peace we had unraveled quietly at first, and then all at once. We barely saw him again, and when we did, he was either too exhausted to speak or too angry to connect.

E.D, now promoted to clinic manager, became his obsession. Every phone call between them was laced with shouting, blame, and rage. Yelling became a daily ritual, background noise we learned to live with, like the constant ticking of a bomb, no one knew how to disarm.

The home I once tried to build into a sanctuary became a battlefield. Not with fists every day, but with doors slammed so hard they shook the walls, with objects thrown, with a presence that could silence a room before he even spoke.

Our children learned to listen for footsteps. To read the temperature of his voice. To measure their breath. The storm was no longer just inside me. It was all around us.

It began with episodes of rage over the smallest things. A simple request like "Can you pay the electricity bill?" could ignite a storm.

"Don't ask me for money! I'll see it and take care of it!"

So, I stopped asking. I quietly placed the bill on the table where he usually sat. That too enraged him.

"Did you put this here just to piss me off?"

It didn't matter what I did. It was always wrong.

Eventually, I stopped mentioning the bills altogether, until the electricity was cut off. Sometimes for days. We sat in the dark while he slept in the clinic, enjoying the comforts we no longer had at home. The disconnect between us deepened.

He disappeared more and more. Our evening dinners with his brothers S.S, once routine, turned into embarrassing scenes. We'd prepare everything, waiting for him to arrive. But he wouldn't show. Or he'd walk in three hours late, while everyone sat around a cold table, starving and silent.

Even food couldn't bring us together anymore.

His father W.S had remarried, and my ex-husband was the last one in the family to accept it. His bitterness lingered like a shadow, and nearly a year into their marriage, we were finally allowed to visit W.S again with the rest of the family. But even that small step toward normalcy didn't last. During one of those visits, a disagreement erupted between my ex-husband and his father. It escalated so quickly, so violently, that he nearly hit him. We were kicked out and banished. And just like that, we were cut off again. Isolated.

For over a year, we couldn't attend any family gathering if W.S was expected to be there.

His refusal to respect anyone's time, space, or feelings eventually spilled over into the entire family dynamic. The house that once felt like a family home became a prison of exclusion. No one really knew what was happening behind our closed doors. We became invisible.

And in that invisibility, his violence intensified.

His outbursts became more frequent, more destructive. Breaking things in the house became his first response to anything that upset him. Ironically, the days he worked long hours were our moments of peace. When he walked through the door, the entire atmosphere changed. We all started walking on eggshells. We never knew what would set him off.

He became careless and disrespectful in ways that felt both cruel and deliberate. I was expected to clean up after him silently. If he left the bathroom floor soaked or left clumps of hair across every surface, it was my job to erase the evidence without a word. Everything outside of work had become beneath him.

He did nothing at home. Never helped, never showed up. Even when I gave him weeks of notice so he could attend our children's school events, he still never came. Not once.

He made sure his presence was known only when it was feared.

I can't really pinpoint when the physical abuse started. It's all so blurry. It didn't happen in a single moment. It seeped in, slow and thick, like fog. By the time I realized what it was, I was already choking on it.

But I remember one day with perfect clarity. Not because it was the worst day. Not because it was the loudest. But because on that day, the illusion finally cracked.

It was 2013, just before my birthday. We had his family over for dinner, and after they left, I stayed up until two in the morning cleaning, scrubbing the bathrooms, the kitchen, and the floors. Every surface sparkled. I was exhausted, but there was a quiet satisfaction in the work. I wanted everything to be perfect so I could rest the next day.

The next morning, I woke up feeling feverish. My body ached as if I had been hit by a wave. I lay in bed and cried quietly to myself, tears I didn't even try to stop. No one would notice. No one ever did.

I forced myself out of bed and walked to the bathroom.

And there it was.

Sesame seeds. Everywhere.

Scattered across the floor. Smeared across the bathtub. Stuck to the soap and the loofah. Coating every surface like confetti after a cruel joke.

It felt deliberate. Calculated. Spiteful.

I stepped out of the bathroom and saw him. I don't remember how I found the courage to speak. My voice came out soft, almost apologetic.

"I stayed up so late cleaning. You could have been more considerate."

That's all I said.

And just like that, he exploded.

One sentence, one whisper of a boundary, was enough to shatter his illusion of control. His rage ignited instantly. He tossed the table in front of his chair and without warning struck the dresser. The mirror shattered. Splinters of wood and shards of glass exploded across the room like shrapnel. The sound was sharp, violent, final.

I stood there frozen. Not out of fear. Not yet. Out of disbelief.

Because until that moment, the violence had been contained. Silent. Internal. Invisible. But there it was now, in the air, on the floor, on my skin, a truth I could no longer talk myself out of.

The glass on the ground felt like a map of my life. Fragmented. Reflecting nothing clearly. Cutting everything it touched.

And still, I didn't scream. I didn't run. I didn't fight back. I just stood there, watching the version of him I had spent years justifying, explaining, defending, and loving disappear before my eyes.

The illusion didn't crack that day. It shattered.

It was the first time the damage moved from inside me to the world around me. But it wouldn't be the last.

I grabbed my car keys and drove. I drove until I couldn't see through my tears. I pulled over and cried until my chest was hollow. There was nothing left to pour out.

When I finally returned home, he was there. The kids were in their rooms, quiet and withdrawn. He never apologized. Not once. Instead, he justified his rage, saying I had ruined a surprise he had planned.

He told me he had been invited to a dental conference in New York that June and that I was supposed to go with him. It was meant to be a gift, a romantic gesture. But, according to him, my complaints had spoiled it.

And yet, I let it go. Because I wanted to go to New York.

There was just one catch: I had to pay for my own ticket. So, I saved every penny I could spare. I even sold one of the two gold jewelry pieces my mother had recently gifted me. I scraped together just enough for the flight and two thousand dollars for expenses. That was mine.

We spent five days in New Jersey before the conference began. He claimed he had money but couldn't access his account. The card wouldn't work, he said. So, he took the money I had saved, all of it, promising to return it as soon as we got home or once his card was activated.

He never did.

For years, he bragged about that trip, how generous he had been, how he let me buy whatever I wanted. But he always forgot the part where he took my money. The money that paid for everything.

Still, I refused to let him ruin it for me. That trip was magical. In spite of him.

I remember standing beneath a towering skyscraper and seeing a dentist's name in bold letters across the glass. I tilted my head back, looking up at the sky, and I meant it when I wished one day his name would be there. That he would have his own building. His own legacy. Because he was talented. No one could deny that. And I wished, with all my heart, that we would finally have enough so he wouldn't have to work that hard. So maybe, just maybe, he'd come home. For once.

That trip to New York was the turning point.

After we came back, the shift was undeniable. It wasn't sudden but it was steady, like a slow leak in the walls of everything I had built.

E.D was no longer just a background figure. Her presence grew quietly but forcefully. She was now part of every conversation, every plan. At one point, my ex-husband casually mentioned that she was jealous of me for going to New York with him, and that he would be taking her to the next conference. She was being elevated. Positioned. Prepared.

Then the money followed.

Suddenly, all his earnings flowed through E.D. If I needed the household allowance, I had to ask her. I had to ask my ex-husband's secretary for my children's daily allowance while she had all the income and the checkbooks at her disposal. Then came the car. He bought it for her, for work, he said. And just like that, she became part of our daily life even without stepping into our home.

My ex-husband and I no longer spent time together. We had become strangers who shared the same address. Most days, we only crossed paths on the stairwell, me and the kids leaving for school, him just returning from the clinic, bleary-eyed and distant. We were living parallel lives, moving in opposite directions, as if we no longer belonged to the same story.

And then, slowly, I felt myself being replaced. Not by a lover or a romantic affair, but by a presence that had become more important to him than I was. His interest in her was strictly work-related, or so he claimed. But the lines between professional and personal blurred until her influence eclipsed mine. She held his time, his trust, his money, and even his schedule. She became his gatekeeper, his right hand. And I became invisible.

It all came to a head during a snowstorm.

A blizzard was sweeping through the city, and people were urged to return home, to be with their families. Streets were closing, schools shut down, and neighbors checked in on one another. It was instinctual, human, and protective.

But not him. He looked out the window at the falling snow, picked up his coat, and said flatly, "I don't want to be stuck at home." And he left.

While the world huddled together for warmth and safety, he chose to be anywhere but with us. He went to the clinic, to his work, to his control, to whatever gave him more comfort than his own family.

E.D was praised for everything the clinic achieved. The success I had helped build was forgotten. I became the voice of complaint, the ungrateful wife. I didn't appreciate the bliss I was in; he told me.

But I was tired.

I turned inward. I gave myself to my children, my son B.S, my daughters N.K.S and T.K.S My energy, my love, my focus. They became my sanctuary.

For the next six months, we were no more than ghosts sharing the same space. Strangers bound by silence and shared history. The air between us was thick with avoidance, every corner of our home holding something unsaid.

I stopped asking questions. I stopped needing answers.

I found condoms in his laptop bag and said nothing. I saw more tucked inside his desk drawers at the clinic, carelessly placed, visible to anyone who looked. His employees noticed. I noticed. But I buried the truth beneath a fortress of denial.

Because infidelity, real infidelity, was unthinkable. A sin. A betrayal so deep it couldn't be undone. And no matter how broken or brutal he became, he still wore the costume of a religious man. He prayed. He fasted. He told others how to live with righteousness. I convinced myself, relentlessly, that he would never cross that line. He was a man of prayer, a man who spoke of God between his cruelties. Surely, I thought, physical sin was a line even he wouldn't cross.

I ignored the signs not out of blindness, but out of survival. I needed to believe the version of him that made life bearable, the illusion that kept me upright.

It wasn't until years later when everything between us had already collapsed that he finally confirmed what I had buried under layers of denial.

"Every time I came home and took a shower after work," he said, his tone almost bored, "it was to wash off the smell of sex."

The words didn't just break something in me. They exposed what had already been broken. And though I sat in silence, I realized I had always known.

The last straw came when my son B.S developed a rare and terrifying allergic reaction, one that mimicked anaphylactic shock every time he played football. Within a single month, I rushed him to the ER multiple times. His face would swell, his lips balloon, hives would explode across his skin like flames, and his breathing would grow tight and shallow. It was urgent every single time.

That year, he received a scholarship to one of the top schools in the country. I was so proud. He began attending there while I stayed behind at my school with my daughters N.K.S and T.K.S One day, I was in the middle of teaching when I was called out of class for an emergency phone call.

It was my ex-husband.

He told me our son B.S was having another allergic reaction and needed to be rushed to the ER immediately. I panicked, told the school to pull the girls from class, and ran to the car. My hands were shaking as I turned the key in the ignition. I assumed he couldn't go because he must have been in the middle of surgery.

I wish that had been true.

Halfway through the frantic drive, he called again. Not to check on our son, but to check on me. To see if I was going. And then he shattered me.

"I'm home," he said flatly.

He had been at home the entire time. Fifteen minutes away from our son's school. While I, forty minutes out, was racing through traffic, risking everything to get there. He had chosen not to go. Chosen not to lift a finger for his own child.

What kind of father does that?

That moment was the beginning of the end. The moment I realized, fully and irreversibly, that I had to get out.

I picked my son B.S up and spent six hours with him in the hospital. Tests. Treatments. Stress. We came home exhausted. And he was still there. Sitting. Indifferent. He didn't ask what happened. Didn't care about the diagnosis, the reaction, the blood work. Nothing.

Later that night, after we had settled in, I told him it was over. That our marriage wasn't working. That I wanted a divorce.

And that was the first time I was raped.

He said, "We haven't had sex in six months. If you're not sleeping with me, you must be getting it somewhere else."

Then he grabbed me.

He pinned me face-down to the mattress. I froze. I couldn't move. My body became like a statue, stone and silence, as he violated me until he was done. No love. No emotion. Just punishment. Just power.

When he finished, he got up, grabbed his bag, and left for the clinic like nothing had happened.

The door clicked shut and the silence was heavier than any sound.

The next day, he took his recliner and some clothes and announced he would be living at the clinic until he found an apartment. Then he did what he always did best: he played the victim. He spun a story that made me the villain. Told everyone I was the heartless wife who threw him out, the cruel woman who betrayed the great man he believed himself to be.

But I knew the truth.

And this time, I won't forget it.

Chapter 13: The House Without Walls

E.D continued working with him after he moved to live in the clinic. During that first week, she stayed with him until midnight every night until her husband gave her an ultimatum: quit or lose her marriage. She quit and chose her marriage.

With her departure, the source of all our destruction seemed to vanish. His friends and even the elders in his family came to me one by one, pleading. "Take him back," they said. It was a bad image for him to be living in the clinic. He was a successful dentist who should be living at home with his wife and children. He never looked for a place to stay; most probably never intended to.

And I said yes, like I always do.

But he didn't return out of love. He came back out of convenience, carrying vindication instead of remorse. And once he was settled, he called E.D back. He asked her to return to work and promised her husband that things would be different this time, that his aunt, a dental hygienist with experience in the United States, had joined the clinic, and that his wife would never have to stay late anymore.

Then one day, he came home with his aunt. He had visible bruises. When I asked him about it, he said he had been in a car accident. But something didn't add up. His story kept shifting, and his behavior was strange.

His aunt had been working with him and E.D for about a month by then. The very next day, she sent a message to both of us, resigning. Then she came to visit me in person.

She looked me in the eyes and said, "He's a drug addict. I know it. I've seen it before. My daughter went through it. I've seen the white powder, the signs, the residue. And that secretary, the office manager, the mistress, she's not just a distraction. She's, his supplier. She's the most important person in his world. She's the one holding all the strings."

The accident, it turned out, wasn't an accident at all. His aunt told me the truth: he had been attacked by E.D's husband and brothers. Why? Because he had assaulted her husband and beaten him viciously after the man slapped her for coming home late again. It was a whirlwind of violence and dysfunction, almost too surreal to grasp.

But she insisted. She had witnessed enough. Then she looked me in the eyes and said, "Call him. Ask him what she gives him that you never did."

So, I did.

Without hesitation, he said, "Can you pretend to be sick so a psychologist will prescribe you Ritalin and then give it to me?"

I said, "Not in a million years."

And that's when the beast returned.

He snapped. A storm of screaming, cursing, and name-calling poured through the phone. And then came the threat: "I'm coming home to teach you a lesson."

His aunt turned to me, her voice calm but firm. "You can't stay here. It's not safe." And just like that, she gathered me and the children and took us to her home.

As soon as we arrived, my phone rang. It was him, screaming like a madman. He had broken into the apartment, claiming he had forgotten his keys. And then the threats began.

"If you're not back in thirty minutes," he said, "I'll start breaking things. One TV every five minutes. And if that's not enough, I'll burn the apartment down."

I knew he meant it because I had seen what he was capable of. Every five minutes, like clockwork, my phone buzzed with another photo. A shattered TV. A broken dining chair. Destruction, piece by piece, as if he were counting down to something darker.

By the time his aunt and I returned, the scene was devastating. All four of our televisions, paid for by my hard work, were destroyed. Two dining chairs lay splintered. The front door had been damaged and shoved out of its frame. The neighbors had gathered outside, drawn by the noise.

But one yell from him and they scattered. Grown men and women ducked behind their doors like children hiding from a storm. No one intervened. No one dared.

I stood there defenseless and trembling while only his aunt stood between me and whatever violence he was ready to unleash. He threatened to beat me beyond recognition.

Then, as if that wasn't enough, he demanded I kneel. He made me kiss his shoes while begging for forgiveness. He ordered me to call myself degrading names while calling E.D a saint.

And I did. Out of fear. Out of exhaustion. Out of complete psychological surrender.

He accepted my forced apology. And then, just like that, he moved back in.

Soon after, he came to me with another manipulation, even darker than before. He claimed E.D's family, her husband and brothers, were planning to kill both of them for suspected adultery. It would be an honor killing, he said. And only I could stop it.

He begged me to vouch for her. "You're the wife," he said. "If you swear there's nothing going on, they'll believe you. Just say she's innocent. Say she's only dedicated to her job. Say she's the only one who understands the clinic's finances."

And I did. Driven by fear. Brainwashed into obedience. I sat in a room filled with her family, her husband, her father, her brothers, and I said exactly what he told me to say. I swore she was innocent. That there was nothing between them. That she was simply a loyal, overworked employee.

Then he jumped in.

"I have more faith in her virtue and morals than I have in my own wife," he said.

And I sat there, burning on the inside, numb on the outside, while he destroyed what little was left of my dignity.

They believed every word of it. E.D was back at work the next day, this time with a significant raise.

Later that night, at home, I tried to speak to him. Not to argue. Just to explain gently how hurtful his words had been. How saying he had more faith in her virtue than in mine had shattered something in me. I kept my tone soft, barely above a whisper, tiptoeing around his ego like it was made of glass.

He looked at me with that familiar, unhinged glare and said, "You're divorced."

Just like that.

In Islamic law, a verbal divorce carries legal weight unless it was spoken in a state of extreme rage. He stormed out, raging like a force of nature, and in his fury, he ripped the front door out of the wall, frame and all. No tools. No struggle. He was strong as a bull and just as wild. He went back to living in the clinic for a few weeks.

And somehow, in ways I still can't fully explain, he found his way back into my life again. Divorce was no longer on the table. Or maybe, more truthfully, it had been pushed off the table by the weight of everything else crashing down around me.

My sister M.G was finalizing her divorce from an abusive husband. She was smart and got out within the first year of marriage, thankfully with no children. But even then, he had stolen all her gold and money. She had to obtain her divorce by absentia, as if even the courts didn't expect her to get justice face-to-face.

My brother E.G was also struggling in his marriage, drowning quietly, unable to catch a break. So, when I looked for support, I was met with weariness. My mother, worn down by seeing too many of her children suffer, said the one thing I will never forget:

"Stay with him. Live as if he doesn't exist. Even if he brings a woman home while you're there, ignore it."

And so, I tried. I stayed. I tried to live around him, through him, past him. I tried to survive in silence. For as long as I could.

Chapter 14: No More Pretending

This time, he knew I was broken. He could do whatever he wanted, unchecked, unchallenged. I was living in a kind of self-induced hypnosis, functioning like a robot. He said "go here, I went. Do this, do that, I obeyed. No questions. No resistance. Just mechanical submission, day after day, for what felt like forever.

And for a while, I convinced myself it was fine. That as long as he had his drugs, he would be calm. That peace, no matter how toxic, was better than chaos. I believed that keeping him satisfied meant keeping us all safe.

But then his demands shifted. They took on a new form. He was no longer just the center of the household. He had become our god. His needs towered over everyone else's. His comfort, his desires, his ambitions were sacred. Above all.

At one point, someone expressed interest in investing in his clinic, a real opportunity. But he was too disorganized to follow through. So, he turned to me. He locked me inside the house. Took my phone. My car keys. He would not let me go to work until I finished building his presentation.

For three days, I worked nonstop on his project. I researched, wrote, and designed. I gave it everything I had. But when it came time to finalize it, he was too lazy to complete it himself. And when the opportunity slipped through his fingers, he looked me in the eye and said, "It's your fault."

As a reward for my submission, he arranged for us to spend a month at a countryside ranch during the summer break. It was a stunning place peaceful, open, and quiet with a beautiful pool and sunsets that painted the sky like fire. The children and I were genuinely excited. For a brief moment, it felt like things were starting to look better.

He drove us there, then returned to work during the day and came back at night. The evenings were calm, almost dreamlike. We swam, laughed, and watched the sky melt into gold. It felt like life was finally offering us something soft.

One day, he told me he wanted to invite his clinic team for a barbecue, just a day to unwind. I agreed. It sounded fun. We ordered food that needed to be picked up nearby. When everyone arrived , the dentists, the technicians, and of course Ema. D he casually decided he would go pick up the food. With her.

It felt inappropriate. Unnecessary. But his absence created an unexpected space.

While he was gone, the people who worked with him pulled me aside. The air shifted. And then, quietly, they began to tell me what had really been happening. One detail left me frozen: the clinic was closed the following Thursday, and only he and Ema. D were scheduled to go in, supposedly to work on the financial books. The rest of the team had the day off.

I tried not to overthink it. The rest of the afternoon passed smoothly, and I pushed the doubt aside. I did not want to ruin the calm we had finally found.

But then Thursday came.

He left that morning as if it were any other workday. At around one in the afternoon, I called to check in. He told me he was in the middle of oral surgery and would be home late. Then, strangely, he started talking loudly on the phone to the very doctors who were supposed to be off that day. Something felt wrong.

The same doctor who had warned me earlier called that day to confirm the entire team was off. No patients. No surgeries.

Just him. And her.

I waited for him to come back. The moment he saw my face, he knew. I was upset, but I approached him cautiously, choosing every word with care, careful not to ignite his rage.

"We're supposed to be working on our relationship," I said softly. "But you weren't honest with me. You didn't have surgery today. You were alone with her."

And in an instant, he transformed. The calm mask vanished, replaced by fury.

"How dare you call me a liar?" he screamed, his voice echoing off the walls of the quiet ranch.

He grabbed me by the collar of my shirt and shoved me backward toward the balcony railing. There was a three-story drop behind me, and suddenly, half of my body was dangling over the edge. He was still screaming; his face contorted with rage. My heart thundered in my chest. I did not scream. I could not.

Then, like a flash, my son B.S came running.

He threw himself between us and pushed his father back, breaking his grip and shielding me with his body. And just like that, the roles reversed.

"Your son laid his hands on me!" he shouted. "This is what you wanted. To turn my children against me. To make me look bad in front of them."

He was not sorry for nearly throwing me over the edge. He was only sorry that someone saw it.

That night, I slept on the sofa.

At around five in the morning, I opened my eyes and his face was right in front of mine. Inches away. His breath against my skin. His eyes were wild, unhinged. Before I could move, before I could even register what was happening, he started punching me in the skull. Not hard enough to leave visible bruises but calculated. Deliberate. Each blow sent a wave of pain through my head, deep and throbbing, enough to make me cry out.

I wept silently, curled up on the cushions, trembling under his fists.

Then, for the first time, he said it out loud.

"I'm going to kill you."

He grabbed my phone, hurled it at me, and shouted, "Go ahead. Call 911. By the time they get here, I'll have cut you into pieces."

He kept talking calmly, almost amused, while he hit me again and again. His words became a rhythm, timed with each blow. My body stiffened, my thoughts scattered, fear choking the edges of my consciousness.

Then the children woke up. And like a switch had been flipped, he stopped.

He stepped back and transformed. Just like that. His tone turned cheerful, his smile wide, his demeanor suddenly soft. Like nothing had happened. Like the nightmare was mine alone.

I realized, in that moment, I was not just living with an abuser. I was living with a monster who knew exactly what he was doing.

From that night on, I knew I was no longer safe.

But I did not have a car, and he had gone to work like nothing had happened. I did not want to ruin the girls' day, but my son B.S already sensed something was wrong. He had seen too much. He felt the shift in the air.

That evening, my ex-husband came home late and said he wanted to sleep early. We all tried to keep things quiet. Calm.

Then, somehow, a small kitten slipped into the house. We heard her meowing softly in the corner. He told us to get her out. I did not know where she was. My daughters Nat.K and Tat.K were asleep, and only my son B.S and I were quietly searching. The kitten was scared, hiding. He asked again, this time louder. "Get her out."

We still could not find her.

Without warning, he jumped out of bed, grabbed a bat, and started slamming it against the wooden furniture, sending thunder through the walls. The poor kitten, startled by the noise, ran into view.

And with a single swing, he hit her. Killed her instantly. Her tiny body collapsed. Blood splattered across the floor.

He turned to me with a cold, dead look in his eyes and said, "This is what will happen if you don't do what I say." Then he handed me a towel and said, "Clean the blood. Get rid of the body. I don't want the girls to see."

And I did. With shaking hands. My son B.S watched in silence, frozen in horror.

And in that moment, something in me died too.

I became a good girl. The obedient wife. I did everything he said. I kept my voice soft, my eyes down, my thoughts hidden. I survived.

In early 2015, my parents moved to the United States. I longed to see them, my only refuge, but I knew better than to expect kindness when asking. So, I asked carefully. "Can I visit them?"

He said yes. "If you pay for your own tickets."

That year, his career reached a new height. His reputation as a dentist had begun attracting wealthy patients, powerful names, and deep pockets. Eventually, he convinced one of them to invest $140,000 into opening a new clinic in a more prestigious location. The investor delivered. He found a beautiful dental clinic for sale at just $70,000, a rare chance to buy it outright and build something solid.

But he did not. Instead, he gave $3,000 to E.D.. He bought himself an extravagant motorcycle and then, without discussion, told me I would no longer be working at the school. "You'll work for me now."

I was terrified. But I did as I was told, remembering my mother's words.

We had moved into a new apartment because he did not want to live in the place where he had once been kicked out. As if changing walls could erase history.

One day, he had me running errands nonstop. I was exhausted, but I knew better than to complain. After I finished, I passed by the clinic to drop off some paperwork. He was on the phone, his back to me. I quietly placed the papers on the desk and stepped away.

That is when he turned and said, "Why are you looking at my phone?"

"I wasn't," I replied, confused. "I swear I wasn't."

He narrowed his eyes. "Are you blind?"

"No."

"Did you see me holding my phone?"

"Yes, I saw you holding it."

That was enough.

The slap came out of nowhere, so forceful that it shattered my sunglasses and tore the skin beneath my eyebrow. "You're a liar," he snarled. "You swear to God while lying?"

Blood stung my eye. My ears were ringing. I stood there frozen. Then he said he was tired and told me to drive him home. We picked up sandwiches on the way. He stayed in the car while I went upstairs. Minutes passed. Too many. Then the phone rang.

"I was waiting for your call," he said, calm and venomous. "You need to apologize for lying."

One day, I was with him at the clinic. He had recently purchased a machine for nearly $20,000, but the company had never delivered on their promise to provide training. Frustrated, he asked if it could be returned. I gently told him, "The lawyer said we can't."

That was all it took.

There was a hose nearby, part of one of the dental machines. He grabbed it, folded it over, and began whipping my legs and thighs with it. The sting was sharp, immediate. I tried to run, but he caught me and shoved me against the wall.

"I'm begging you," I cried. "You have daughters. How would you feel if someone did this to them?"

"If they deserved it," he said without hesitation, "I'd be on his side."

I looked at him, horrified. "Then I will make sure they never deserve it."

That must have struck a nerve, because the next moment, his hands were around my neck. He began choking me, tight and relentless, until everything around me faded to black.

I woke up on the floor, an oxygen mask over my face, and him crying. He was crouched beside me, tears falling, apologizing over and over, kissing my hands and begging me not to tell the children what had happened. As always, I agreed.

He reminded me that I would soon be visiting my family, that some time away would do me good, that I would come back refreshed and ready to continue this life. It sounded like kindness. Like comfort. He even helped me buy gifts for my parents and siblings. I had become the perfectly obedient wife again, so in his eyes, I was safe to reward.

My bags were packed. My flight was the next day.

That evening, I bought one last gift, then picked up food and took the kids to have dinner with him at the clinic. It was almost peaceful. We laughed. We ate together. I almost allowed myself to hope.

But he never came home that night. I waited. I called. He said he had lost the keys to his truck. Again and again, he claimed he was searching, but time slipped by and I missed my flight. Hours later, he walked through the door and said casually, "They were in my pocket all along."

I asked him to rebook the flight. He said fine, as if none of it mattered. He went to work and returned home like everything was normal. Then he asked me to go for a drive with him. I agreed. Why would I refuse? Things had seemed calm.

We drove in silence for a while, and once we were away from any populated area, he pulled over and parked. Without warning, he reached over and hooked his finger inside my left cheek, yanking my face down toward the armrest.

"This is called the fishhook maneuver," he said coldly. "Don't even think about resisting."

I was pinned. Paralyzed.

Then came the punches fist after fist against my face. Blood poured from my nose. He screamed that I had cheated on him. I had not. I never had. I never would. Then, with twisted logic, he spat, "I cheated. And God said in the Quran that cheaters end up with cheaters. So, if I cheated, that means you did too. God doesn't lie."

I cried and begged to go see my family. I said nothing else. What else was left to say?

When he was done, he handed me a bottle of water and told me to wash the blood off my face. He did not want the kids to see. By then, they were already used to their clumsy mother who fell a lot.

I went home and collapsed into bed. It was dark. The kids were already asleep. I prayed the night would pass quietly.

But he came home drunk. He staggered toward me and demanded my passport. I pointed to the drawer. He reached inside and accidentally grabbed his own. The moment he realized the mistake, he exploded.

He ripped both of my passports- Jordanian and Iraqi - apart. He destroyed my driver's license, slashed my debit card, and burned my cash right in front of me, watching it curl and blacken into ash. Then, as if none of it were enough, he sat down and said coldly, "I'm going to sleep now. When I do, kill me. Because if I wake up, I'm killing you. I've been planning how to do it all day."

I did not cry. I did not speak. I just sat still, watching him drift off, breathing shallow and ragged.

Once he was fully asleep, I moved in silence. I gathered every torn document I could find, what was left of my identity. I took my car keys and left.

I drove to the home of the wealthy Sheikh who had once asked for my hand in marriage. His family had always shown me kindness. I had kept in touch with them, maybe out of intuition, or maybe out of hope that someone in this world still saw me.

That night, I asked for their help.

They took me in without hesitation and immediately began helping me secure new documents. Destroying a passport is a felony, and if it had not been for their powerful connections, I may never have been able to leave the country.

I got a new phone number, hoping to sever all ties, but somehow, he found a way in again. He hacked into my Facebook account and found a message from my mother urging me to seek their help if things got very bad, that they would help me come to the United States. That was all he needed.

Using my son B.S's phone, he contacted me. At first, he played the role of the kind, desperate husband, begging me to come back for the girls. I had left so suddenly, I never got to say goodbye. I never had the chance to explain. The only one who knew the truth was my son B.S.

I did not want to leave my daughters behind, but I was paralyzed with fear. I could not trust him anymore. I had become the sole target of his physical abuse, and in a cruel way, that was what kept my daughters N.K.S and T.K.S safe.

My son B.S, barely a child himself, became their protector. Whenever his father's temper rose, or he began acting in ways no father ever should, my son B.S would quietly lock his sisters in their room. He shielded them from the shouting, from the sounds, from the truth of what was happening. Because of him, they were spared from the violence that lived inside our home.

When his false kindness did not work, he turned to threats. He said, "I know where you're staying. I know how conservative they are. I'll go to the police and tell them the

Sheikh's wife is holding you against your will. Or they can pay me $50,000 and I'll let you walk away."

That night, the family I was staying with pulled some strings and had a new passport issued for me. They booked me a first-class ticket and bought me a few outfits. They pressed some money into my hand, hugged me tightly, and sent me to my family.

Leaving my children the way I did shattered me. I could not eat. I could not sleep. I felt like I had abandoned them, and the guilt was unbearable.

A few weeks later, my son B.S started calling, pleading with me to come back. He told me that his father had given him his word, that he would not harm me, that I would be safe. He said things would be different.

And I wanted to believe him.

I missed my children so much it hurt to breathe. This was not the life I wanted - being apart from them, hearing their voices only through a phone. Then came the messages, voice notes and pictures of him holding the phone, sent to my mother. He said he did not want his kids to grow up without their mother. He said he would do anything to fix things, and if they could not make it work, they could separate peacefully. He promised I could stay with the kids.

And for a moment, I let myself believe it. I thought maybe, just maybe, losing me had been the wake-up call he needed.

My father and my brother Ed.G were against me going back. They knew his patterns and they knew how this story could end. Years earlier, my brother Ed.G had bought an apartment and registered it in my name. Before I left, they insisted I give him power of attorney to sell it. They knew, just as I did deep down, that if I returned without protecting that property, my ex-husband would manipulate me into giving it up.

While waiting for the power of attorney to be certified, I distracted myself with hope. I started shopping for my children, buying them clothes and toys, little things I imagined would bring smiles to their faces when I returned. I took pictures of the gifts and sent them, imagining our reunion, desperate to believe we could still be a family.

Once the documents were finalized, my brother E.G flew to Jordan ahead of me and sold the apartment. I followed two days later, full of love, longing, and a fear I refused to name.

I was excited, clinging to the image of my children's faces lighting up when they saw me, when they opened the gifts, I had so lovingly chosen for them. For a moment, I let myself believe this return would be different.

As I boarded the plane, my phone rang. It was him. His voice was cold, detached, emotionless.

"Where are you?"

"I'm on the plane," I told him. "Waiting for takeoff."

Then came the sentence that turned my blood to ice.

"How stupid were Saddam Hussein's sons-in-law when they believed he wouldn't kill them after they betrayed him?"

And then he hung up.

I sat there frozen, the words echoing in my skull like a death sentence. I could have left the plane. The doors were still open. There was time.

But all I could think of were my children. Their eyes searching for me at the airport gate. Their little hands opening their gifts. Their joy. Their love.

I could not abandon them. Not again. Not like that.

If I was walking into death, then so be it. At that moment, their smiles were worth dying for.

I cried the entire eighteen-hour flight, not knowing if I was flying toward an embrace or an ambush. I did not know if I would ever get off that plane alive.

And yet, that was only the beginning. That was the first time I ran away.

I did not know then that in just six months, I would be running again.

Only this time, there would be no return.

Chapter 15: Six Months in Hell

The plane took off, and I stared at my reflection in the window. Tears streamed down my face without pause. As I looked at her, that broken woman, I wondered, would this be my last night on Earth? Would I get to see my children at the airport... or did he have other plans?

I cried openly. Strangers noticed the fear in my eyes, the desperation carved into my face, the quiet collapse of someone barely holding on. But that face... it wasn't mine. Not anymore. That was her face, the woman I used to be.

After nearly eighteen hours in the air, we had a brief layover in Istanbul before continuing the flight. When the plane finally touched down, my heart was a battlefield of emotions: hope, happiness, fear, excitement, and dread all colliding inside me. As I walked through the arrival gates, I spotted him. He was standing there... with my children.

For a moment, a wave of relief washed over me.

He brought the kids.

He won't hurt me in front of them.

That thought became my shield as I moved closer. The moment I saw them, I rushed forward and pulled them into my arms as if it had been years. We were all crying tears of reunion, of aching joy.

All of us... except him.

He stood motionless. His eyes were ice cold. As if whatever soul had once lived behind them was long gone. We drove home to the new apartment. Unopened boxes still littered the floor from our recent move. He allowed me to spend a few moments with the children.

I opened the bags and handed them the gifts I'd brought from abroad.

Their eyes lit up. That look, their joy, was priceless. But then, with a sharp tone, he ordered them to their rooms and forbade them from speaking to me.

I entered the bedroom, bracing myself.

What kind of punishment would he choose this time? But... nothing.

The sofa from the guest room was now shoved into our bedroom. The bed, once a place of rest, was littered with tangled electric wires, loose screws, rusted nails, and leaking batteries. There was nowhere to sit, safe to exist.

He looked at me and said coldly, "You came back to destroy me. And you've already succeeded. Everyone knows you ran away from me." I tried to explain that most people thought I had simply gone to visit my family. They didn't know I had missed my flight. No one would have ever guessed the truth unless he had told them.

We didn't talk much that night. Silence filled the apartment like a fog. We went to bed without a word, each of us on edge for different reasons.

The next morning, I wasn't allowed to speak to my children. I sat alone in the kitchen while he stayed in the bedroom. The kids weren't even allowed to come near me, let alone sit beside me. I could hear them whispering behind closed doors, but I was off-limits. Like a stranger in my own home.

Later, once he was fully awake and alert, he summoned me to the bedroom. Without emotion, he said he hadn't been able to work during the weeks I was away. He claimed he was too ashamed to face people because I had humiliated him.

"If you want to reconcile," he said coldly, "you'll give me your brother's apartment." It was a demand, not a request. But my father and brother had anticipated this. My brother had already flown to Jordan ahead of me and sold it before I returned.

I told him the truth. "My brother sold it before I returned," I said. "If you don't believe me, go check."

His eyes darkened. "Then give me the deed to your father's apartment, the one we live in." Again, I stood my ground. "It's under my father's name," I said. "I don't have the power of attorney."

Every answer was the result of careful planning, acts of protection by the men who still valued my safety, even from afar. Right then, as if to underscore his desperation, his phone rang. It was the previous owner of the motorcycle he had recently bought. Apparently, he had missed two payments. The voice on the other end was firm and unbothered: "If you can't afford it and won't pay me, I'll take it back."

That was enough to send him into a raging storm. He exploded, screaming so violently that spit flew from his mouth. Everything, according to him, was my fault. The bike. His shame. His debts. And now, I had to fix it.

"You'd better find the money," he shouted, "even if you have to beg in the streets!"

Thankfully, my brother had given me three thousand dollars from the apartment sale. I hid one thousand in a secret place, my only safety net. Then I handed him the other two thousand, more than enough to cover the missed motorcycle payment. He snatched the money and stormed out on his bike. He didn't come back until well past midnight, drunk, high, and reeking of the streets. I had no idea where he'd been or what he had done. I only knew the monster had returned. Or never left.

The next day, the bike owner called again, still waiting for his money. And just like before, my ex erupted. "This is your fault!" he screamed again.

"But I gave you the money," I said, stunned.

He dismissed me like a fly. "I had a more important debt to pay."

Again, the man called, this time with finality in his voice. He said he was on his way to retrieve the bike himself.

My ex-husband peeked through the window and saw two police cars parked near the building. Assuming they had come to assist in repossessing the motorcycle, he panicked.

Without a word, he leapt on the bike and sped off toward the clinic. Moments later, the bike owner arrived at our apartment. I told him honestly, "He just left. He's headed to the clinic." The man nodded, called my ex-husband, and followed him there.

Ten minutes later, my ex-husband called me. "Stay on the phone," he said coldly. "You need to hear this."

What follows still makes my skin crawl.

The man had arrived. But before he could speak, my ex-husband attacked him. I heard all the blows, the grunts, the cries. The man begged him to stop, pleading for his life. "Please don't kill me," he cried. But my ex-husband kept hitting him again and again. And in between each strike, he barked into the phone: "Don't you dare hang up!"

I listened helplessly for fifteen agonizing minutes, while a man was beaten within inches of his life. Only then, when the begging had drained to a whisper, did he let him go.

He summoned both me and his secretary to come immediately to the clinic. To say I was terrified would be an understatement. Even his secretary called me beforehand, her voice shaking. She was summoned too. We went together.

The moment we arrived, he unleashed his fury, screaming at both of us. His rage filled every corner of that clinic like a toxic gas. Then he told her to leave. And just like that, I was alone with him.

As soon as the door shut behind her, he turned to me with eyes full of hate. He kicked me hard right on the shin. I crumpled to the floor. Before I could catch my breath, he began kicking me in the back, over and over, targeting my kidneys. "I hope you get internal bleeding and die," he spat. Then he threw me out of the clinic.

I stumbled home, bruised, broken, and afraid to cry. But things were already spiraling. The family of the man he assaulted had contacted his relatives. They were accusing him of attempted murder. The victim was in the hospital. In response, his brother suggested filing a counterclaim to protect the family name. But it was already night, and they couldn't do anything until morning.

When he returned home, he was holding a large bottle of highly concentrated absinthe. He told the children to go to their rooms. Then he led me into the bedroom and locked the door behind him. He dragged me into the bathroom, sat me on the toilet, and began slapping me across the face.

"Make a sound," he warned, "and I'll kill the children."

I didn't make a sound.

The slaps kept coming, but the pain didn't register anymore. It felt like I had left my body. I hovered somewhere above, watching myself bleed from the nose, detached, weightless, numb.

Eventually, he let me out of the bathroom. He started drinking. After every few sips, he'd strike me with the bottle again and again on the back of my head. Then he called his brother, raging at him in fury. But his brother wasn't intimidated. So, he called his father. With venom in his voice, he said: "I always knew you were gay. That you got paid to have sex with men." Then he sent a mass message to everyone on his phone saying his father was available to sleep with men for money.

But he wasn't done.

The second message was about me. He told the world I had cheated on him.

All the while, he kept hitting me in the back of the head with the bottle. I didn't pass out; he made sure of that. Each blow landed with precision, not to knock me unconscious, but to keep me awake. Alert. Aware. Trapped in the moment. He wanted me to feel every strike, to see the pleasure in his eyes as he watched fear take over my face.

My body reeled from the blows, but I stayed silent, still floating. When the bottle was empty, he pushed me onto the bed, forced my legs apart, and tried to shove the bottle into me. He said, "I will mutilate you. You'll be no good to anyone when I'm done with you."

I don't know how, but I managed to push him off. He stumbled, furious, then grabbed a utility knife, the kind with all the small screwdrivers and scissors folded inside, bulky enough to cause real harm. Before I could move, he struck me in the forehead with it. Blood poured from the wound, warm and relentless.

I was alone in the room with him. And I knew that if I screamed, if I made a single sound, he would turn his rage toward the children. So, I stayed silent, trembling, the blood trickling down my face, praying they wouldn't wake up, praying he would stop.

Eventually, I must have blacked out. I don't know when he passed out from the alcohol, but at some point, he did too.

When I opened the bedroom door, I found my son… kneeling on the floor.

He wrapped his arms around me and whispered, "I was trying to hear your voice… just to know if you were still alive."

The next morning, his brother came to the house, planning to take him to the hospital to file a counterclaim against the man he had beaten. He looked me in the eye and said, "I'm just happy you're alive. We thought he was going to kill you."

They knew. His family knew. They all knew what he was capable of and still, they did nothing to protect me. After everything I had done for them. After all the years I stood by them like one of their own. I cooked for them, took care of them, defended them, covered for them. And when I needed help the most, when their brother was trying to destroy me, they watched in silence. That betrayal carved something out of me I can never get back.

But he wasn't finished.

He told his brother he wouldn't go to the hospital just yet; he had a few things to "take care of" first. He called his secretary and told her to come to the house immediately. Then he stepped into the bathroom to draw himself a bath. When she rang the doorbell, her face was as pale as death. She was trembling, just like I had been so many times before.

Then, from inside the bathroom, he called out to me: "Give her my towel and my boxers so she can dry me."

My hands shook as I carried the things to her. She said nothing. She took them. And she obeyed.

I stood there in stunned silence, watching another woman walk toward the man who had just brutalized me the night before, a man who was now naked and summoning her, as if I didn't exist. It was humiliating beyond words. Not just because it was a declaration of her being his mistress, but because she was stepping into that room while I stood there stripped of whatever dignity I had left.

It should have filled me with rage. But all I felt was sorrow. Because I saw it in her eyes the fear, the helplessness, the shame. She wasn't there because she wanted to be. She was there because she had no choice. I don't know what he had over her. Naked photos? Secrets? Fear of exposure? Whatever it was, he had her under his thumb. It wasn't even her workday. Her family had come to visit, and she told him she couldn't leave.

His reply? "I don't care if you're having sex with your ex-husband. If I say come, you stop and come."

And for some reason, she did. Because the threat behind his voice left no room for refusal.

Still, he wasn't done. He needed to fix another prescription for Adderall. He was snorting 120 tablets a week, using different doctors and patient names to feed his addiction. This particular doctor had refused to write any more prescriptions. So, he ordered both me and the secretary to go to the clinic. He parked outside and made her keep him on the phone so he could hear every word, every breath.

The moment we walked into the office, the doctor recognized her immediately. His face tightened. Without a word, he picked up the phone and called building security. Two guards entered and stood behind us, silent and ready, before he even addressed us.

She tried to speak calmly. "My doctor sent me to pick up a prescription for him."

The doctor's eyes narrowed. "No. Absolutely not. He's an addict." She hesitated, then pulled a folded piece of paper from her pocket, something my ex had told her to give him only if he refused. She handed it to the doctor.

His expression changed as he read it. His hands started to shake. Then his voice rose in fury. "This is a threat! He said he knows what my son looks like. He said he knows what school he goes to!"

And then, chaos. Before anyone could react, the door flew open. My ex-husband burst in, fists swinging, eyes wild. He struck patients in the waiting room. He shoved his way past the guards and into the doctor's office. He hit the secretary. He screamed like a man possessed. It took both security officers and the doctor himself to wrestle him out of the clinic.

We followed him downstairs. His voice was sharp and commanding. "Get in the truck," he barked. We obeyed.

He drove like a madman, swerving from lane to lane, clipping parked cars on both sides. He was destruction in motion. Then he slammed the truck to a stop and turned us on, hitting both me and his secretary. The chaos must have drawn attention. Moments later, the police caught up with us. He resisted arrest, thrashing like a wild animal. They subdued him, finally, and threw him into the back of the squad car.

Before they arrived, his secretary managed to slip away and took her own car. But I wasn't so lucky. I was taken with him to the police station.

To my horror, they placed us in the same room. I sat frozen while he spun a lie so twisted I could barely believe it. When they asked why he attacked the doctor, he said, "He was sexually assaulting my wife. I heard him on the phone attacking her, so I rushed in to protect her.

He spoke so convincingly. So effortlessly.

But one officer watched me carefully. While the other kept him distracted, he leaned toward me and whispered, "Is that true?"

I shook my head. Just barely. No. The officer understood. He turned back to my ex-husband and asked, "Do you have children?"

"Yes," my ex-husband answered.

The officer gave him a pointed look. "Then maybe you should keep your wife out of this. She doesn't need to be dragged through the police station and the courts. That won't be good for your reputation or your kids."

That was when my ex threw himself backward in his chair and faked a fainting spell. He even urinated on himself.

The officer glanced at me and said quietly, "Don't worry. That's typical addict behavior. We've seen this before."

And to my immense relief, they took him to jail. I was finally free to go home. But I had no phone. He had taken mine the moment I returned from my trip.

He found another way to reach me, calling one of our neighbors and asking them to convey his message. He needed money and a change of clothes. But I had nothing. No money. No car. No way to call anyone. So, I took my son's hand, and we walked. We walked to the nearest relative, his uncle's house. When I told him what had happened, he barely blinked. He said he'd "take care of it tomorrow." But then he looked closer. At the bruises. The dried blood still caked into my hair. Silently, he handed me some cash, just enough for a cab to get home.

The next morning, the knock came. It was the landlord. He had heard about the arrest. "You need to leave before the weekend," he said. "The rent was never paid."

I stood there numb, wondering how we'd survive. But for once, a tiny piece of luck was on my side. I still had my father's apartment, and I still had the one thousand dollars carefully hidden from the money my brother had given me. Whatever I had left barely covered the movers. When we arrived at my father's old apartment, the electricity had been cut off due to unpaid bills. That night, we had no choice but to sleep at his brother's house. To his credit, his brother paid the electricity bill and bought us a few groceries. The next day, we returned to the apartment. There was no comfort. Just survival.

Meanwhile, his family met with the victim's family in a tribal court. To avoid legal prosecution, his father and brother agreed to cover the cost of the motorcycle and all the hospital bills. In exchange, the charges were dropped.

He spent over a month in jail.

During that time, with the help of my own family, I filed for divorce. I tried to get my job back, but school had just started and my position had already been filled. We had no income. No security. We lived on scraps. His brother handed me a few dollars here and there, enough to buy bread or milk.

I tried to stay strong for the children, but every day chipped away at me.

Then, near the end of the month, his brother came to see me. He sat down and said, "Jail changed him. He's not the same. He's clean now. He's remorseful. He's begging to see you."

His brother had always been a straight man. Reliable. Honest. So, I trusted him. And against the screams of my own instincts, I agreed to visit him in jail.

He looked thinner. Calmer. Soft-spoken. Remorse dripped from his words like honey. He promised me everything I had ever needed to hear. That it would be different. That he had changed. That he just wanted a new beginning for us, for the kids.

And once again… I fell for his lies. We told the girls he had been on a trip to Bora Bora. We even bought them toys and said they were from him. That first night back, he was a man transformed. He cried. He held my hands. He spoke of dreams, of starting fresh. It was almost beautiful.

Then came the ask. He gently brought up the idea of me withdrawing my retirement pension. He said he wanted to grow the business, that if I supported him, we'd finally have a real shot at building a future.

I hesitated. My heart was torn between hope and fear. In the end, I said yes.

I withdrew around fifteen thousand dollars. I secretly transferred three thousand to my mother, just in case I needed an emergency exit. But I gave him the rest, about twelve thousand dollars. He even wrote me an "I owe you" note. He kissed my hands. He said I had saved him. That he would never forget this.

Less than a week later, the money was gone. And so was the kind man.

The moment the account hit zero, he laughed in my face. He said the money I gave him wasn't "even enough to wipe his ass."

Eventually, he began frisking me before I could use the bathroom. I wasn't allowed to lock the door. Every movement, every blink, every breath became suspicious. If I blinked while he was speaking, he'd freeze and ask, "What did that mean? Why did you blink? What are you trying to say?" If I sighed, he'd keep me up all night interrogating me. Over and over. Night after night. Until I no longer knew how to be.

I can't even count how many nights I sat on the edge of the bed, exhausted and hollow, trying to remember how to blink… without being punished.

Some nights, the torment didn't end until morning. Other nights, it began after midnight. He would call me from his clinic, demanding I bring him food. His office was surrounded by restaurants, anything he wanted a few steps away, but no, he was too important to get his own food.

One night, I was completely broke. I told him I had no money. He scoffed. "If you were a good wife," he said, "you'd find a way. Now I'll stay hungry, because of you."

His cruelty was never about logic. It was about dominance. He would stare at me coldly and say: "Say it. Say your mother is a bitch." Not because I had provoked him, but because he wanted proof of complete submission. Proof that no one came before him, not even the woman who gave me life.

If I refused, he'd fly into a rage. His eyes would go wild, unhinged. He would hit me in the head with his knuckles, yelling louder and louder, repeating the demand. Over and over. Until I broke. Until I said what he wanted.

One day, I got a call from my youngest sister. Her voice was angry, confused. "Are you on drugs or something? Are you insane?"

"What are you talking about?" I asked.

She said she had received a series of texts from me the night before saying I was cutting ties with her. That she should never contact me again. That every time she visited, she had been with my ex-husband. That I was disgusted by her.

I was stunned. I had been asleep. Then he walked into the room while I was still on the call. I turned to him and asked, "Did you send those messages?"

He shrugged and said coldly, "I didn't want her to visit anymore. Every time I see her, I lust after her."

My sister heard it. She exploded, yelling at him, calling him an addict and a pervert. That was all it took. She became his new enemy. And just like that, he made it my war to fight. He demanded I call her back and say the words. And then block her forever.

I refused. He was relentless and wouldn't let me be, until I obeyed.

My youngest daughter had been struggling with her homework, and she needed my help, but I was stuck at the clinic, at his mercy. Every time I tried to leave, I said, "She needs me. She asked for help."

His reply never changed: "She's not important. I am."

He kept me there until midnight. By the time I got home, she was asleep. Tears on her face. She didn't want to go to school the next morning because she didn't know how to do the work. Because her mother hadn't been there to help.

He came home shortly after sunrise. Saw her tears and slapped me again and again across the face. "You're not good enough to be a mother."

Something inside me snapped. For the first time, I fired back.

"Son of a bitch," I said.

He froze, stunned. No one had ever spoken to him like that. Especially not me. But I wasn't done. "For the record," I said, "your mother is no better than mine."

He snapped. Grabbed a fistful of my hair and dragged me down the hallway, my body scraping against the floor. Our daughter saw it happen and ran to help me. He turned on her and pushed her down. She stumbled backward and ran to her room, crying. That was it.

With every ounce of strength I had left, I kicked him hard. He stumbled, and for a moment, I thought I had broken the spell. But instead, he stood there and began his next act of cruelty. And that was the first time he truly confessed to committing adultery, the very sin I had convinced myself his faith would never allow.

He looked me straight in the eye and said, "One time I brought a woman to our bedroom. She was ready. But then I saw your picture on the wall and told her to leave."

He said it with pride, as if that were mercy. As if restraint in the face of betrayal could erase the fact that he had desecrated the very space where love was supposed to live.

Then he smiled. "You should thank me," he said. "You should build me a statue for being so loyal."

He wasn't joking. He meant it. He wanted praise for restraint, for sin, for humiliation. He demanded gratitude for not crossing the line he had already obliterated.

And in that moment, I realized there was nothing left to reason with. No part of him that could still recognize right from wrong.

"I cheated. So that means you must've cheated too. That's God's law of balance."

Then the slapping started again. "Confess!" he screamed. But I had nothing to confess. My conscience was clean. I had never betrayed him. That didn't matter.

"If you didn't cheat before," he hissed, "then cheat now. I want to see it. I want to watch another man in front of me."

The room spun as he unleashed fantasy after fantasy, twisted thoughts of using my body as a prop in his perversions. He started naming names. The young doctor at his clinic. The salesman I once met for clinic brochures. The coworker who once put a hand on my knee years ago, long before this. He threw them at me like accusations.

In a moment of desperate sarcasm, I said, "Fine. I cheated on you with Christian Grey from Fifty Shades of Grey."

He was actually pleased. He grinned. And for a while, he dropped it. Like a child distracted by a new toy.

Then one morning, he left for work. Before he left, he asked for his favorite meal. I cooked it, hoping maybe it would make the day quiet. But he never came home. Later, he called me. Drunk. Rambling. Laughing. He was at a friend's house. I asked him to come home. He refused. Instead, he invited me to join him. Something in his voice was perverted and disgusting, so I hung up.

His brother went to see him at the clinic the next day and simply said, "Things are not working out between you and her. Divorce her."

There, my ex-husband told him, "I'm acting like this because she cheated on me."

His brother didn't buy it. "Then divorce her," he said: "I can't live without her," my ex-husband replied.

"If she really cheated on you," his brother said again, "then you must divorce her. That's what any man would do."

Then he turned on his brother too. "Why do you want me to divorce her?" he snapped. "Because you love her? Because you want to be with her?"

That was it for his brother. He called me, his voice shaking. "I can't be involved anymore," he said. "Not after what he just said." This was a man who had flown F-16s for eighteen years, a military instructor trained to face death in the sky. He told me that in nearly two decades, he had never brought his service weapon home. But now, he kept it by his bed. "Because I don't know what he's capable of anymore," he said. "I'm terrified of what my own brother might do."

That was the last straw for me too.

I changed the locks.

I contacted the same lawyer my family had hired for my first divorce attempt. She listened carefully and told me, "Go to Family Protective Services." And I did.

When they reached out to him, he exploded. He cursed at them, threatened them, and every time they called again, his rage escalated. He started threatening to kill me again.

Even while I was trying to reclaim my life, the fear never left. I would be at home, trying to find peace, and my son, innocent, hopeful would be playing games on my phone. That's when the messages would come. From his father. "I saw your mother kissing a man," one said. Another: "She's at a hotel with him."

And then the nightmare inched closer. One morning, at six a.m., he showed up at the apartment. I refused to let him in. So, he banged on the neighbors' doors, screaming for everyone to hear. "Come out! Come and see the whore who lives in this building!"

Another time, he asked to take the children for a day. And I couldn't say no. Only my son returned that night. "I'm keeping the girls," he said coldly. "You'll never see them again." He had taken them to live with one of his patients. Days passed and I didn't know where my daughters were.

Then, mercifully, a woman called. She gave me the address. I went. And I brought my daughter's home.

The threats kept coming. The accusations. The humiliation. The stalking.

I thought of killing myself because I saw no way out. I slept with a knife under my pillow because I feared he would break the doors again and kill me. I was desperate and hopeless.

Until my son saved me in the dark hallway of our apartment, his eyes brimming with tears. He took a deep breath and said, "I'm sorry, Mama. I asked you to come back. I promised I would protect you. But the way things are going… he's going to kill you. Or hurt you in a way you can never recover from. He's too strong. I can't stop him." Then he looked at me, his voice breaking. "You have to leave. You have to save yourself. Maybe one day we'll see each other again. But at least… at least I'll know you're alive."

That was it.

I had nothing left to hold on to but survival. I still had the tickets I had booked the year before, meant for a simple family visit. Now they were my escape route. I was going back to Houston.

As my lawyer moved forward with the divorce, she contacted him directly. And he turned his threats on her. He threatened her and her family. But she wasn't going to take it. She looked me in the eyes and said, "Let's go." My lawyer filed for a restraining order.

That's when the death threats changed tone and became something far more terrifying. He told me that during his month in prison, he had made friends. Murderers. Drug smugglers. Men who, in his words, "wouldn't mind killing you for a tooth filling." He said he wouldn't even need to pay them. "They'd do it for fun," he said. "For the thrill. I wouldn't even need to cover the cost of the bullet." Then he added, casually, like discussing the weather, "I already have someone waiting for you. The second you step outside that building, he'll kill you. The only way you're leaving is in a body bag."

From that day forward, I never left the house alone.

My lawyer, who had started as a professional, became something more. She had known my parents through a close mutual friend. And now she became my protector. She drove me to court appearances. She escorted me through crowded streets. And finally, she walked me through the airport gates. All the way to the plane. She didn't just represent me. She shielded me.

And just like that, six months after I had returned to try to hold my family together... I was running for my life. Again, but this time, I had no doubts. There was nothing more I could have done. Nothing I didn't try. No corner I left unexplored in my desperate attempt to save a marriage, a home, a name.

This time, I wasn't leaving out of fear of shame. I was leaving out of certainty. This time, my children knew. They had seen it, some of it. They had lived through the edges of the storm. Maybe one day they will understand. Maybe they would forgive me.

Because this time, leaving wasn't a choice.

It was life or death.

Chapter 16: The Woman on the Sofa

I had survived.

That was the only word for it. Not thrived. Not landed. Not begun again. Just survived.

I had crossed an ocean with two bags and the clothes on my back, leaving behind twenty years of a life, my furniture, my apartment, my children, my identity. And now I was here, in Houston, Texas, sleeping on my parents' living room sofa.

Their apartment was a two-bedroom. My parents shared one room. My brother and his eldest son, Al.G, shared the other. There was no room for me. There was only the sofa and the unspoken understanding that I was grateful to have it.

My father woke before dawn every morning to pray. That part I understood. What came after was harder. He would finish his prayers, settle into his chair, and turn on the television. Loud. Loud enough to hear from the curb outside. Loud enough to reach every corner of that small apartment, including the living room where I lay pretending to sleep, staring at the ceiling, wondering how I had arrived here.

I didn't say anything. I had no right to. This was his home. I was a guest in it, a grown woman, a mother of three, a pharmacist, reduced to a guest on her parents' sofa.

Those first months were the strangest of my life. I had escaped something that was trying to kill me, and yet I did not feel free. I felt untethered. Like a kite with a snapped string, no longer trapped, but no longer held either, just drifting in whatever direction the wind decided.

I cried most of the time. Not always loudly. Sometimes it was just the slow leak of tears that came without warning in the shower, in the car, in the middle of a sentence. Sometimes I talked to myself. Full conversations, out loud, processing things I had no one to say them to. I caught myself doing it once in the parking lot of a grocery store and stood very still for a moment, wondering if I had finally lost my mind.

Maybe I had. A little. That is what years of abuse will do. It does not just bruise the body. It rewires the brain. It teaches you to doubt your own perception, to question your own memory, to believe that the chaos you lived in was somehow your fault, your failure, your flaw.

I had spent years inside that rewiring. And now, sitting in the quiet of a Houston apartment with no one screaming at me and no danger lurking behind closed doors, I did not know how to be still. The peace felt unfamiliar. Almost suspicious. I kept waiting for something to go wrong.

My brother had a coffee shop not far from the apartment. On the days when the walls closed in, when my father's television became too loud and the sofa felt too small and the weight of everything I had lost pressed down too hard,

I would go there. I would sit in the corner with a cup of coffee and watch people move through their ordinary live, laughing, arguing, scrolling their phones, existing without the particular heaviness I carried everywhere.

It was my only escape. My brother never asked too many questions. He just let me sit there and be.

My first friend in Houston was a woman named Z.T. She appeared in my life the way good people sometimes do quietly, without fanfare, as if she had simply decided that I needed someone and appointed herself to the role.

She came almost every day. She would knock, or call, and take me out for a drive, for coffee, for nowhere in particular. Just out. Just moving. Just away from the sofa and the television and the weight of the four walls. Once, she took me for a manicure. It was such a small thing. But I remember sitting in that chair, watching someone tend to my hands with care, and feeling something crack open in my chest not pain exactly, but the memory of what it felt like to be treated gently. I had almost forgotten.

My mother did not approve of Z.T. She was single, living alone and in my mother's world, a single woman living alone was a warning sign, a bad influence, a door best left closed. She made her disapproval known in the way mothers do, not always with words, but with silences and looks and the particular tension that fills a room when something is being said without being said.

I ignored it. Z.T was the only person making me feel like a human being. I was not giving that up.

My mother gave me $2,000. It was everything and nothing at the same time everything because I had almost nothing, nothing because the list of what I needed it for was longer than the money could reach.

I had transferred what remained of my pension before leaving. Combined with my mother's gift, I had just enough to move, barely, through the first steps of building a life from scratch.

I bought a used car. It was not pretty, but it was mine the first thing in years that was entirely mine. I paid a fee for one of the licensing exams I would need to eventually reclaim my career. I put a down payment on an immigration lawyer, because without legal status, none of the rest of it mattered.

Every dollar was doing three jobs. I stretched each one as far as it would go and then stretched it a little further, the way you do when you have no choice. My lawyer told me about a women's shelter on Montrose that offered group therapy sessions. I went.

I am not sure what I expected. I sat in a circle with other women, women who had come from different lives, different countries, different kinds of pain and I listened. And then, slowly, I began to talk.

What the therapy gave me was not comfort, exactly. It was something sharper and more valuable than comfort. It gave me language. For the first time, someone put words around what I had lived, words like cycle, and pattern, and trauma bonding. Words that turned the chaos of my marriage into something that could be understood, something that had a shape.

I learned about the abuse cycle. How it moves in stages, the tension building, the explosion, and then the part that destroyed me every time: the honeymoon. The apology. The flowers. The man on his knees with tears in his eyes, kissing your hands, swearing it would never happen again.

I used to believe him. Every time. Not because I was stupid. Because I was human. Because the man who appeared in the honeymoon phase — tender, remorseful, achingly familiar — was the man I had fallen in love with. And I kept believing that version was the real one. That the rage and the cruelty were the aberration. That if I could just be patient enough, careful enough, good enough, that man would stay.

He never stayed. He was never real. He was a tactic.

Sitting in that circle on Montrose, I finally understood that I was not mentally ill for staying. I was not worthless for accepting the abuse. I was not weak or broken or deserving of what had been done to me. I was a woman caught in a pattern specifically designed to keep me exactly where I was.

That understanding did not heal me. But it stopped the bleeding.

Meanwhile, across the ocean, my ex-husband continued his campaign.

When my daughters called me, which was rare, and only allowed under his supervision, he would sit beside them and instruct them. I would hear his voice underneath theirs, low and steady, telling them what to say. And they, because they were children and he was their father and they did not know any better, would say it.

"We hate you, Mama."

"You are a bad mother."

I would hold the phone against my ear and listen to my daughters' voices carrying his words, and I would remind myself that they did not mean it. That they were being used. That none of this was their fault.

I said it to myself over and over. Some days I believed it.

He broke the phone I had bought my son before I left, so that my son could not reach me without going through him. For a while, we found ways around it, borrowed phones, brief messages, and stolen minutes of connection. But the lines of communication were always fragile, always at his mercy.

What most people did not know was that my children had no real home to speak of. Their father had never bothered to rent an apartment. Throughout our marriage, he had always lived rent free in apartments I paid for, or in the home my father gave us. When I left, he moved what remained of our family into the clinic itself. That was where my son lived. That was where my daughters slept. A dental clinic, not a home.

About ten days after I left, my son was there when his father was with a patient. The phone rang. His father called out to him to answer it.

My son answered it. He was doing what he was told.

It was my divorce lawyer on the other end.

When his father came out and learned who had called, something shifted in him. This was not a coincidence in his mind. This was a betrayal. His own son, scheming against him, collaborating with the enemy.

He threw my son out.

My son went to his grandfather's house. The next morning, he found his clothes on the doorstep. Packed in a trash bag. Left there in the night like something discarded.

That was the message. That was the farewell from a father to his son.

I found out through a message on a borrowed phone. I remember reading the words and feeling a particular kind of helplessness that has no name, the helplessness of a mother who cannot reach her child, cannot stand between him and harm, cannot do anything except exist thousands of miles away and know that her leaving, however necessary, had a cost.

My son found somewhere to go. He always did. He was stronger than anyone his age should have to be, because I had left him no choice.

I carried that guilt like a stone in my chest. I carry it still.

But I kept moving. Because stopping was not an option.

I studied. I attended therapy. I drove my unremarkable used car through the streets of Houston and learned the shape of a new city. I sat in my brother's coffee shop and watched the world go on. I let Zi.T take me for drives and once, for a manicure, and I tried to remember that small kindnesses were still kindnesses, even when everything else was broken.

I was a nervous wreck. I was barely holding together. I was sleeping on a sofa in my parents' living room at forty years old, waking to the sound of a television turned up too loud, sending money I barely had to children I could not reach, trying to rebuild a life from materials that kept crumbling in my hands.

But I was here. I was still here.

And somewhere in Houston, a man I had not yet met was saving $7,000 in an envelope and waiting, without knowing it, for me.

Chapter 17: The Love I Never Knew Existed

I woke up happy today.

Last night, I asked Diaa to visit me in my dreams, and he did.

He was just as handsome as I remember. Broad, muscular shoulders. A smile as wide as the world.

It felt so real, so warm, like coming home.

I didn't want to wake up, but the alarm rang gently yet mercilessly.

The dream faded, and reality settled in. Still, I carried him with me.

And for that, I'm happy today.

The hour-long drive to work and back gives me space to feel released. Alone in the car, I don't have to manage anyone else's emotions. I don't have to apologize for crying or pretend I'm fine. It's just me, the road, and my thoughts.

My mind drifts back through time, revisiting the winding path that brought me here, to this country, this life.

And I wonder: what was the purpose? What is the big picture behind all this pain, all this strength, all this survival?

Under fireworks, under stars, under every broken dream, he chose me.

And I chose him.

I never thought I could love again. It wasn't something I was searching for or even believed was possible. My heart had been broken in ways I didn't think could ever heal. Love had become a foreign language spoken by others beautiful but unreachable to me.

But Diaa made loving him feel as natural as breathing. Being with him felt like stepping into sunlight after years spent lost in the shadows.

At first, it was just texting. I teased him about his name sounding Arabic. He brushed it off with a smirk, insisting he was Canadian with Italian roots. His flawless grammar charmed me. A small detail, maybe, but to me, it meant everything. Words mattered. They were sacred. The way a person used them revealed more than they realized.

Eventually, our texts turned into late-night phone calls. I still remember the first time I heard his voice, warm, confident, thoughtful. It made me feel safe.

During one of those early calls, he paused and said, "I want to tell you something… but please don't be mad."

I laughed. "Go ahead. I promise I won't be." Then he began speaking Arabic.

I laughed again and kept saying I knew it, I knew it I had sensed it all along. But there was something tender about the way he offered it up, like he was handing me a secret part of himself.

We spent more than a month just talking, before we finally met in person.

Coffee at Starbucks. I had just finished studying and was exhausted but excited. He arrived in a bright green T-shirt and a baseball cap, even more handsome than his photos, fit, vibrant, magnetic. There was strength to him, a quiet intensity that drew me in without effort.

We didn't spend much time together at first, just that one coffee in January 2017.

But everything shifted by the end of -February, when my brother's ex-wife, Zozo, arrived from overseas with my nephew Alex . They stayed in our family apartment until Zozo found a modest two-bedroom place nearby.

That small apartment quickly became my sanctuary. Living with my family again felt like being trapped in a time capsule. Like I was eighteen all over again. They judged the clothes I wore, questioned where I was going, asked when I'd be back. I was forty-one. A woman who had raised children, run a household, survived a war of a marriage and still, I was treated like a rebellious teenager. They even warned me not to go out with my brother too often, whispering that people might mistake him for my boyfriend.

Zozo's apartment became my escape. She gave me space. She gave me air. Half the week, I stayed there in that modest apartment tucked away from the world.

And without meaning to, that space became something sacred. It was in that quiet, overlooked corner of the city where our love was conceived, not in grand gestures or declarations, but in cups of coffee shared on borrowed time, in whispers that dared to dream beyond the lives we were trapped in.

That apartment became our refuge. A place untouched by judgment, by noise, by the ever-watchful eyes of a world that wouldn't have understood us. It was our breath between suffocations. Our warmth between winters.

It wasn't just a roof. It was where I remembered what it felt like to be seen. To be wanted without being owned. To be held without being hurt.

In that apartment, love wasn't loud, but it was real. And for the first time in years, I didn't feel invisible.

Zozo welcomed Diaa instantly, as did my nephews A. G and Alex , as new immigrants, Zozo and my nephews were overwhelmed with paperwork, appointments, and errands in a system that felt foreign. There was always something that needed to be done, always a form to fill, a ride to give, a process to navigate.

And Diaa, without a second of hesitation, jumped in to help. He didn't wait to be asked. He didn't do it for recognition. He simply showed up, driving them to offices, waiting in long lines, helping in every way he could. To him, kindness wasn't a performance. It was instinct.

He became their anchor in a sea of uncertainty, their steady hand in a new and dizzying world. And watching him the way he gave without expecting anything in return. I saw the man I had always dreamed about but never believed existed.

And somehow, he was mine.

Little by little, I found myself needing him more and more. Not for grand things, but for the quiet reassurances the way he remembered the smallest details, the way he listened when no one else did.

He didn't just show up for me. He showed up for everyone, even remotely connected to me. For Zozo. For my nephew. For anyone who held a piece of my heart. It was as if he loved everyone who loved me. As if, by caring for them, he was caring for parts of me I didn't even know needed tending.

He wasn't trying to impress. He was simply being. And in being, he healed. He healed what others had broken without even knowing it.

There was a swimming pool right in front of Zozo's apartment. We would sit beside it for hours, talking about everything and nothing, the kind of conversations that felt effortless but carried weight beneath the surface.

One evening, as I reached for a cigarette, he snatched the pack from my hand with a grin.

"I dare you to get them back," he teased, his eyes dancing with mischief.

I leaned in, laughing, reaching and in that moment, our bodies brushed. Just the lightest contact. A spark.

But it felt like lightning tore through both of us, a jolt that struck something raw and buried. In an instant, a fire ignited, quiet, fierce, and far too real.

I pulled away, startled by the intensity. He didn't say a word. Just smiled and handed the pack back, as if he hadn't felt the world shift beneath our feet.

Above us, the full moon floated in the velvet sky, casting silver light over water, skin, and secrets we weren't ready to name.

The fire had been lit. And though we said nothing, we both knew nothing would ever be the same again.

That night, something shifted. Something unspoken. Something undeniable.

The very next evening, his voice came through the phone different. Raw. Quiet. Trembling at the edges he said I must tell you something.

Then came the confession. He was married. He had been sleeping in his daughter's room for eight months, still living under the same roof as his wife. He had told me he was divorced when we first started talking, and the truth landed like a blow.

My heart shattered. As much as I wanted him, as deeply as my soul had begun to recognize him, I told him we had to end it. I could not be the reason a marriage ended. I wouldn't break a family would and I could never be someone's mistress.

He pleaded with me to listen. Told me the marriage had died long before I ever entered his life.

Then he sent a photo, his face slashed and bruised. The aftermath of a fight. His wife had been enraged over a necklace that their divorced neighbor had brought him to fix, as he worked in a jewelry store, and that was all it was. An act of kindness. Nothing more. But her rage would not be reasoned with, and what she left on his face told the whole story.

I didn't know the full picture then. It was only after he was gone that his friends came to me with the rest of it, the things he had been too private, too protective, too dignified to ever say himself.

She had always been like this. Her jealousy so consuming it had no logic, no ceiling, no mercy. She had slowly cut him off from his own world, his culture, his language, his people. He was Lebanese, warm and rooted in community, in music and food and the kind of laughter that fills a room and she was Pakistani. Over the years, the differences between them had curdled into control. She didn't just want him. She wanted to contain him. To erase the parts of him that existed before her.

When arguments erupted and he tried to leave the house to let the air clear, the way any reasonable person would, she would follow him. To the Walmart parking lot. To wherever he drove to find a moment of peace. She would pull up beside him and continue the fight, refusing to let it end, refusing to let him breathe. There was no escape. No cooling down. No door to close between them.

They had been living like strangers, trapped in a house that hadn't been a home in years, a prison made of broken trust and quiet hostility.

His friends also told me something else, something I will carry with me for the rest of my life. They said that before me, he was simply existing. Going through the motions. Surviving for his daughters sake, but from the moment I entered his life, something in him came alive. They said he only started living when he met me.

And I understood that completely. Because he did the same thing for me.

But there was something else I understood, something that went deeper than love. I believed him when he described what his life had been, not because I was naive, but because I recognized it. I had lived it. I knew what it felt like to shrink yourself to keep the peace. To leave the house just to breathe. To absorb blow after blow and tell no one, because survival sometimes looks like silence. I had run from that darkness myself. And when I looked at the bruise on his face and heard what his life had been, I didn't see a man making excuses.

I saw a mirror.

He told me he had been saving money quietly, secretly, hiding cash in corners, because they shared a bank account and every dollar spent was monitored, every choice questioned.

I loved him. But love alone wasn't enough. I had learned that lesson.

I told him: if that was the truth, he needed to move out and file for divorce. Then, and only then, could we talk again.

He didn't waste time. The next day, Diaa appeared at Zozo's apartment with an envelope in his hand $7,000 in cash.

"I've been saving this, like I told you, "He said. "Please help me. I need a cosigner to get an apartment. I don't have a Social Security number yet. Will you help me move out?"

I understood what he was asking and what it meant. Diaa had come to the United States from Canada and was living here without documentation, his path to a green card rested on his American-born daughter, who would be able to petition for him once she turned twenty-one. I was in a different kind of limbo. I had applied for asylum after arriving on a visitor visa, and while that case remained pending, I had been granted legal authorized stay, the right to live and work while the process played out. It wasn't certainty, but it was ground to stand on. And Zozo, who knew everything, stood quietly beside us both.

I stared at him, stunned. "You barely know me," I said. "What if I take your money and disappear?"

He smiled a sad, beautiful smile. "Then I'd still be happier losing it to you than losing myself to her."

He chose an apartment in the same complex where his ex-wife lived, close enough so his daughters would always know he didn't leave them. He left her.

He asked me to choose the furniture. "I intend to marry you," he said simply. "Pick whatever you like."

I stood there breathless, the woman who once believed love had left her forever, now holding a future in her trembling hands.

We chose every piece together. The apartment filled slowly, lovingly, with the quiet certainty of two people building something real.

It was the Fourth of July. Zozo and I had planned to watch the fireworks at City Centre. We arranged to meet Diaa there, everything was falling into place until my mother invited herself along. Dating was still a taboo, even at forty-one.

So, we pretended. Pretended it was a coincidence. Just a casual run-in in the middle of a crowded night.

Diaa spoke easily with Zozo and my nephew, but between him and me, there were glances. Glances that carried a thousand unsaid things, a thousand stolen moments we hadn't yet lived.

He looked extraordinary that night. A royal navy shirt. A crisp tie. Every detail was immaculate. He looked like he had stepped out of a dream I didn't know I was allowed to have.

When the fireworks began, I tilted my face to the sky, lost in childlike wonder. And then, almost instinctively, I turned.

He was already looking at me.

And in that single, breathtaking instant, the world fell away. The noise. The lights. The crowds. All of it vanished. It was just him and me, suspended in a moment so fragile, so fierce, it felt like the universe itself was holding its breath.

The fireworks weren't just bursting in the sky. They were bursting inside us. Cracking open everything we had tried to contain. Setting our hearts on fire.

And in that one gaze, without a single word, we both knew. There was no more pretending. No more room for secrets. No more escape.

Love had already claimed us.

A few days later, we picked up the keys to his apartment and waited for the furniture we had chosen together to be delivered.

While we waited for the last of the furniture to arrive, his world was about to crack open. One morning, after he dropped his daughters at school and returned home, she was waiting for him. She kicked open the door of his daughter's bedroom- the room where he had been sleeping for eight months- and stood in the doorway with everything she had gathered. She had hired a private investigator. She had photos of us together, my address, my workplace, the details of my past. She knew I had left my children, crossed an ocean, and started over and in her eyes, I had done all of it to steal her husband.

Diaa didn't deny it. He simply said, "Good. Now that you know, can we finally get divorced?"

She begged him to stay, to wait until the girls finished college. But he was already gone. Their marriage had ended the day she clawed at his face, leaving marks that kept him home for two weeks, a wound born of rage and control. And that was before I ever set foot in America. He had left her long before he ever left the house.

That same day, he packed his clothes and his car tools and moved into the apartment.

The day after, he filed for divorce.

He had done everything I asked of him. And so, we could begin again.

One night, we sat together in his car. The sky stretched endlessly above us, glittering with stars. The silence between us was heavy, not awkward, but full. Charged with everything unspoken.

He turned to me, a mischievous spark in his eyes, and said, "I'm going to do something. Don't slap me."

Before I could ask what, he leaned in and kissed me. Deeply. Hungrily. As if he had been holding back a lifetime of longing.

And when he finally kissed me, I kissed him back without fear, without hesitation, without apology.

That single kiss became a language of its own, a promise that stretched across eight years. Every time our lips met, it felt like the first time. Tender, electric, and impossibly alive.

He never needed to say "I love you" though he said it often. Once, he told me he had said it to me in a single month more times than he had said it in his entire life.

And I believed him. Because with him, love wasn't just spoken. It was lived, breathed, and felt in every small kindness. He showed it every single day.

After a small accident left my car out of service for ten days, he insisted on driving me to work himself. Every morning, before the sun rose, he waited outside my family's apartment engine humming, eyes half-asleep but heart wide awake. He never complained about the early hours or the long drive. And every evening, he was there again, waiting, as if those rides were our little ritual, his way of wrapping care around me without needing to say a word.

No complaints. No expectation. Only love.

He kissed me like a starving man finding water in the desert. Each kiss was a vow:

I choose you.

I will always choose you.

One night, while we were still hiding our truth from the world, something funny and unforgettable happened at Zozo's place. I was supposed to be spending the night at my family's house but somehow ended up unexpectedly at Zozo's apartment, so I called Diaa.

Without a moment's hesitation, he jumped into his car and drove over.

A few minutes later, he texted: "Come outside."

Laughing, I replied, "Why can't you just come in?"

"Just come out," he said. "You'll see."

I stepped outside and burst into laughter. There he was, sitting in his car, wearing nothing but boxers. He didn't waste time getting dressed. He just grabbed his keys and ran to me.

That night, we curled up in his car, wrapped in pillows and blankets, creating a tiny world that belonged only to us. He held me close. My head rested on his shoulder, and he whispered, "Having your head on my shoulder... is my heaven."

That continued to be true until the day he took his last breath.

I had never known love like this. I thought this kind of tenderness only existed in movies. But I was living it. I remember pinching myself, over and over, just to be sure it was real.

He played our song "Jesus to a Child" on repeat. And it was our story. Two broken people, once discarded, finding healing in each other's arms.

By September, Diaa had become a daily fixture at my brother's coffee shop and hookah lounge. He would come after work, settle in, and stay. He was the kind of man who drew attention without trying, sharp, warm, quietly magnetic. Every woman who walked through that door noticed him. He noticed none of them.

One evening he arrived after work, dressed sharply, and went straight to Zozo. I watched from across the room as something between them turned into a small, silent standoff. He kept standing up. She kept pulling him back down into his seat. He would rise, fix his collar, smooth his shirt and she would grab his arm and tug. Up. Down. Up. Down. It was the funniest thing I had seen in months.

I crossed the room, curious, and asked what was happening. He looked at me with complete calm and said he was not leaving that night without me.

Zozo suggested he speak to my brother first. So, he did. He sat down with Ed.G and told him plainly: he wanted to marry me. My brother suggested they wait our mother was traveling to Mecca, better to postpone until she returned.

At that exact moment, as if the universe had been listening, my mother walked past the table. She stopped. "Postpone what?" My brother told her. Diaa wants to propose. She looked between them and said, "Why postpone? Let him come before I leave."

That same weekend, Diaa arrived with his friend Akbar at his side and a diamond ring in his pocket. My father listened, considered, and said yes. The moment my father's answer landed, Diaa reached into his pocket and placed the ring on my finger, right there, in the living room, on the sofa that had been my bed since I arrived in Houston. The same sofa where I had lain awake in the dark wondering if I would ever stop surviving long enough to start living.

That sofa held my lowest moment. And then it held this.

My mother traveled a few days later. And then Hurricane Harvey hit Houston.

The storm flooded the streets, cut the power, and trapped us all inside. Diaa was trapped with us at my family's When the electricity went out at my family's apartment, we all went to stay at Zozo's place, but we needed blankets, Diaa knew a friend who lived nearby in the same complex. The two of us walked together through water that rose above our ankles. His friend opened the door, welcomed us in, and gathered what we needed. She was the first person to meet me as his fiancée.

While staying there we helped Zozo's hang a mirror. I held it against the wall, arms up, trying to keep it steady. And then I felt him step behind me. He placed his hands over mine, both of them, gently, completely as if he were holding me and the mirror at once. He didn't say anything. He didn't need to.

I caught the reflection of my nephew's face in the glass. His eyes were wide and bright, lit from the inside. Zozo stood a few feet away, and I could see it in her too, that sparkle that appears when people witness something real.

Seven days. That was how long Harvey kept Diaa at our side. Seven days for my family to see the man I had been trying to describe to them.

My mother had accepted his proposal for reasons that stung, convenience, mostly. If I was married, there would be no more worry about my reputation, no more policing of my clothes or my outings. A practical calculation dressed as a blessing.

But then she got to know him. And so did the rest of them. By the time the floodwaters receded, Diaa was no longer the man I had brought home. He was family. Not because they decided to accept him. Because he made it impossible not to love him.

He always did.

Diaa wasn't like anyone I had ever known. Not like the men who came before. Not even like my father. Not my brothers. Not even my own flesh and blood.

He was my angel. And I was his.

Two broken souls who found something rare, something holy. A love so sacred, so complete, the world itself faded around it.

Nothing compares to him.

Nothing ever will.

Chapter 18: The Other Side of Love

And I had He made home not a place, but a feeling. A heartbeat. A rhythm that matched mine.

Yet, even in the comfort of his love, I carried echoes of my old life. Sometimes guilt would creep in, guilt for feeling joy, guilt for having peace while my children were far away, guilty for receiving love after surviving cruelty. Diaa never tried to erase that guilt. He simply reminded me that it didn't define me.

His presence didn't erase the scars. It just made them easier to carry. Like warm hands over cold wounds, his love softened the edges. Some days, I would catch myself smiling for no reason, humming in the kitchen, dancing barefoot in the hallway. And he would just watch me, eyes filled with wonder, like he couldn't believe someone so full of life had once been so broken.

In July of 2018, just a few days before Diaa's birthday, my divorce was finally certified by the appeals court. It had been issued in March of that same year, but the legal seal of finality brought an unexpected wave of emotions, relief, sorrow, and the strange ache that comes when you officially close a chapter that once held your entire world.

Diaa's divorce had also been finalized that March.

Both of us had walked through our separate fires, and now, for the first time, we were standing on the other side. Free.

His birthday that year was not only a celebration of his life, but a celebration of a new beginning for both of us.

We rented a two-bedroom apartment in the same complex where Zozo lived, the place where our love was born, sitting under the moonlight near the pool. The place we hid from the world and created another world that held only the two of us, another timeline, another reality. It felt symbolic. Almost sacred.

We chose a two-bedroom intentionally. The second room was for his daughters, so they would have their own space during their visits. Their mother made sure the custody agreement was followed to the letter, and Diaa, committed to being present and loving, made sure the girls always felt welcome and wanted.

Life with Diaa was different, profoundly, quietly, beautifully different.

He wasn't like my father, or my brothers, and he most certainly wasn't like my ex-husband. There was no hierarchy, no power play, no expectation of obedience. There was only partnership.

Our schedules were often opposite. I left for work early in the morning while he worked late shifts. I'd return home to find the house clean, the sink empty, the air calm. And on the rare mornings when he overslept and had to rush out the door, he would later apologize for not making the bed with sincerity, as if that small undone task had failed the standard of care he held for us. But to me, the bed didn't matter. What mattered was the intention, the thoughtfulness that ran through everything he did.

When his daughters came to stay with us, he would wake up early to take them to school, and when they called asking for anything, food, medicine, money, he would drop everything and rush to provide what they needed. He never treated parenting like a burden or a favor. It was part of him.

He cleaned, folded laundry, and washed the dishes without ever acting like it was extraordinary. To him, care was love in motion. Service was strength. He was happy serving others not out of obligation, but out of love. And never once did he feel the need to protect his masculinity by holding back. His manhood wasn't threatened by a dish towel or a grocery list. If something needed to be done and he had the time, he simply did it. And if I had the time, I did. There were no unspoken rules. No scorekeeping. No resentment simmering beneath the surface. We were partners in the truest sense, two people showing up for one another, for the home we shared, for the life we were building.

It was a dynamic I had never known. In my past, every act of service I gave was expected, and everything I received came with a cost. But Diaa didn't keep receipts. He didn't wait to be praised or rewarded. He gave because he wanted to.

And for the first time, I didn't feel like I was performing womanhood. I felt like I was living it on my own terms, next to a man who honored it.

I never had to open doors when I was with Diaa not car doors, not restaurant doors, not metaphorical ones either. He opened all of them with quiet confidence, not because I was incapable, but because he believed I shouldn't have to do it all alone.

I never had to stand for hours ironing shirt after shirt, terrified that a missed crease would earn me a scolding. I didn't have to earn his approval through perfection. I didn't live in fear of disappointing him. In fact, Diaa ironed my clothes. He would take the time to smooth every wrinkle with the same care someone else might save for a precious garment. He even dried my body after a shower, gently, lovingly because he teased, "You don't do it right." But behind the humor, there was a tenderness that felt sacred. He found joy in caring for me. Not as an obligation, but as a privilege.

I could go on for days about the little things he did. The gestures that may seem small to the world but meant everything to a woman who had once been trained to believe that love must be earned through sacrifice. Diaa never saw it that way. He'd shrug, smile, and say, "If it's something I can do, and I have the time, why not? You work just as hard as I do. God gave me the same hands and legs, so why wouldn't I help and make your life easier?"

That was the essence of him. He didn't love in grand, performative ways. He loved in the quiet, consistent ways that mattered most.

In his world, kindness wasn't rare, it was standard. Equality wasn't a gift; it was a given. He didn't wait for recognition or praise. He just showed up, again and again, with humility and grace.

With Diaa, I wasn't a wife bound by duty or fear. I was a partner cherished by choice. And in those ordinary acts of care, he gave me something extraordinary: the freedom to rest, to breathe, to exist without the weight of proving my worth.

This way of thinking was new to me. Radical, almost. I had spent most of my life around men who believed that power came from being feared, that love meant control, and that respect was something women owed, never received. Diaa dismantled all of that with a soft voice and steady hands.

I often found myself wishing my son would grow up to be like him, strong in spirit but tender in action. And I prayed that one day, my daughters would find someone who loved them the way Diaa loved me: without condition, without fear, without asking them to shrink.

We went on dates every week. We experimented with new restaurants. We'd slip into a bar and sit close together listening to live music, our fingers entwined under the table. I didn't know I could be that woman, the one who relaxed, who laughed easily, who leaned her head on a man's shoulder without bracing for impact.

For the first time, I could breathe next to someone. I could joke, I could tease, I could speak my mind without filtering every word for danger. I didn't have to walk on eggshells, wondering how my sentences might be twisted or weaponized against me. I never had to apologize for being too emotional, too tired, too loud, or too me.

Diaa didn't just love me. He loved my children. He loved my family. And it wasn't for show. I didn't have to coach him, didn't have to defend his behavior or explain away his silence. He had one face. One truth. The man people saw in public was the same man who kissed my forehead at night and warmed my coffee in the morning.

He was genuinely kind. Honest to a fault. Blunt, sarcastic, generous to the core.

With Diaa, I didn't just feel loved I felt chosen. And that made all the difference.

That same year, I faced another betrayal, one I never imagined would come. This time, it came from a friend I had known for almost twenty years.

She was my neighbor when I married my ex-husband. The friend who exchanged plates with me when I was pregnant. The friend who had seen the bruises, the fear, the humiliation , who knew every detail of the abuse I endured.

When I fled that marriage, I left everything behind. Twenty years of life packed into two bags. I didn't know what my future looked like, whether my ex-husband would destroy everything, whether I would ever return home.

I gave her the keys to the only shelter I still had. My apartment. I told her, "If you can rent it furnished, or if you have a serious buyer, let me know." I trusted her to guard what I had no strength left to protect.

Weeks later, my son messaged me that the lights in our apartment were on. I asked her. She said it was just a plumber doing repairs. A few weeks after that, another message from my son. Again, the lights. This time she said an electrician was working. Then a neighbor contacted me about noises inside the apartment. When I asked her, she said a painter was doing a quick job because a potential buyer was coming.

The excuses piled up like a wall I was too exhausted to climb.

Finally, I asked my son to go with his grandfather and check the apartment. He called me, crying.

"Mom… there are people living here. And there's no furniture. Nothing is left."

My heart stopped.

I found out she had been renting my apartment for months, collecting money as if she were the owner. My memories, my furniture, the pieces of a life I had to abandon gone. And when I confronted her, she didn't deny it. She didn't apologize. She said she was going through "financial hardship" and that as her friend, I should understand.

That was the final straw.

This was a woman who prayed, fasted, wore hijab, the daughter of a judge, raised in the same faith my ex-husband had used to control me. And yet she stole from me with no guilt, no shame.

I felt violated. Robbed. Exposed and helpless. As if someone had ripped open the last safe space I had left.

In that moment, something inside me broke. If the religion she and my ex-husband followed couldn't stop them from betrayal, then what was it worth? I fell into a rabbit hole of doubt, questioning every belief system I had ever known, questioning God, questioning the meaning of faith itself.

And through it all, Diaa held me the way no one ever had. No judgment. No guilt. No forcing me to believe or disbelieve anything. He simply said, "Whatever brings you peace, follow it."

He let me rebuild my spiritual life one breath at a time, with nothing but love and understanding.

After that day, something inside me settled, quiet, cold, irreversible. I made a vow to myself: after I get my children out of there, I would never go back to Jordan. Not for anyone. Not for anything.

The country that once held my childhood, my memories, my innocence now held nothing for me but betrayal. Every path I had walked there, every face I once trusted, felt stained by what was taken from me.

So, I carried my heartbreak across oceans. I carried the lesson. And I carried the truth that sometimes the place you are born is not the place you belong.

But here, far from the place that had wounded me, I found something I never expected, a new life with Diaa. A life filled with safety, softness, and joy. A life where I wasn't walking on broken glass and bracing myself for the coming storm.

Chapter 19: I Will Not Be Defeated by This

We spent a few months wrapped in the warmth of our newlywed life. Then it was time for me to shift my focus, to rebuild not just my heart, but my career.

Diaa had known me when I was unemployed, taking handouts from my brother and family while I waited on the system to grant me permission to exist legally. In the spring of 2017, I had finally received my Employment Authorization Document and got my first job as a pharmacy technician. But after we got married, it was Diaa who carried most of the financial weight. He never once made me feel like I was a burden. Still, I knew I had more to offer. I wasn't just a survivor; I was a pharmacist. That was who I had been back home, and it was who I wanted to be again.

Getting licensed in the U.S. wasn't easy, but it wasn't impossible either. I began to live by a simple mantra: if someone else did it, then I could do it too. I had already taken the first of the required exams back in April of 2017, but life had swallowed me whole, and I never followed through. Now, everything was different. I had stability. I had love. I had someone who believed in me. And I had a new mission: reclaiming the life I once dreamed of, for myself and for my children.

Around that time, my ex-husband was sentenced to a year in prison. It should have felt like justice, like closure. But all I could feel was panic and dread. For a few agonizing days, my daughters' whereabouts were unknown. After his arrest, they had been left behind, forgotten in the chaos. I later learned they had been taken in by an old patient who happened to be at the clinic when their father was taken away in handcuffs. Eventually, their grandfather stepped in and took custody, but those days of not knowing, of imagining them alone, afraid, abandoned nearly broke me.

My son was about to graduate high school. I had dreamed of that moment for years. Every time a graduation ceremony was held at the school where I once taught, I would sit among the parents and cry quietly not from sadness exactly, but from longing. I could see myself there one day, in those seats, as a mother, not a teacher. Watching my son walk across that stage. That dream was stolen from me too. And even thousands of miles away, even with Diaa beside me, that absence sat heavy on my chest.

Even as I sat at Diaa's side, wrapped in the comfort of our life together, a part of me remained shattered. I carried my daughters inside me like a second heartbeat. Every step I took in my career, every book I opened, every sleepless night of studying I did it for them. Because I needed to rise. I needed to become someone who could go back and protect them. Who could bring them forward into a better life.

Diaa understood. He didn't just support my dream he made space for it. He would clear the living room so I could study in peace. He made dinner, did the laundry, and reminded me to take breaks. He never competed with my ambition. He fueled it. He once said, "You've carried so many people. Let me carry you now."

And he did.

All three of my children were now living with their grandfather and his wife. He was a kind man, but he was aging, and he relied solely on his Social Security income barely enough to support himself and his wife, let alone feed three growing children. It wasn't just a temporary solution. It became clear that I had to step in.

I was thousands of miles away, but I couldn't afford the luxury of helplessness. My children needed food. Clothes. A future. And even though I wasn't physically there to tuck them in at night or soothe their fears, I could be the one keeping their world from falling apart financially.

Diaa helped however he could. He wasn't just supportive emotionally; he stood beside me in every way that mattered. But he also had his own obligations: regular child support payments and three growing daughters of his own. Still, he never once said no when they needed something. He never counted dollars when it came to his girls. And watching that - watching him give with such open-hearted generosity - made me love him even more.

But it also meant that I had to rise. I had to push harder, dig deeper. Getting my pharmacist license wasn't just about personal achievement anymore. It was a lifeline for my children, for our future, and for the woman I knew I was capable of becoming.

To say that passing the licensure exam was one of the hardest challenges I've ever faced would be an understatement. The material was brutal, the process isolating, and the pressure unbearable. There were nights I studied until my eyes blurred, my body exhausted but my mind racing. And there was always that voice in my head: they're counting on you. Don't stop.

Diaa was my anchor through all of it. He would massage my shoulders while I leaned over textbooks, refill my tea, quiz me on drug interactions, and remind me that I was brilliant even when I doubted myself. He never let me forget why I started. He never let me give up.

"I believe in you," he'd whisper. And somehow, those four words gave me the strength of an army.

I passed the language exam on my second attempt. That might sound simple, but for foreign pharmacy graduates, it's anything but. The test was split into four sections, each one demanding, and all of them required to be passed together. You couldn't just pass two or three parts and come back later to finish. You had to succeed in every category in one sitting or start all over again. Some candidates took the exam twenty-seven times before finally passing. Others gave up after a few painful attempts, their dreams silenced by exhaustion and cost. I was one of the lucky ones. The stubborn ones. I passed on my second try.

With that momentum, I set my eyes on the NAPLEX " North American Pharmacist Licensure Examination". The final mountain between me and the career I had sacrificed so much for.

When the review book arrived, I was eager... until I opened it. The excitement drained from my body. The textbook was massive, dense, and intimidating. So heavy I couldn't even carry it comfortably. That first night, I tried to study and ended up in tears, overwhelmed by just the index.

But I didn't have the luxury of fear. I took a deep breath, pulled out scissors and binders, and spent the entire next day cutting the book into manageable pieces. I created two giant folders with fifty-six chapters total. Every page I tore and hole-punched felt like a declaration: I will not be defeated by this.

The gap between my training and what this exam required was enormous. I had graduated in 1998 with a five-year pharmacy degree rooted in chemistry, drug formulation, and pharmaceutical properties. The NAPLEX was entirely clinical; patient-focused, decision-heavy, designed for Pharmacy Doctors, a degree that simply didn't exist when I graduated, I studied. Entire classes of medications that didn't even exist when I graduated. Trade names I had memorized in Jordan meant nothing here. And I had never worked a day in retail pharmacy. I was starting over in a field I had been disconnected from for years

It was 2018. I hadn't sat for an exam in twenty years. I was working full-time, caring for a home, holding my marriage together across two sets of children, and carrying the weight of my children's future.

I knew I would need unpaid time off to focus. That meant saving in advance, not just for myself, but to keep sending money to my children. Diaa understood the weight of that decision. He would be the sole provider during that stretch, and he didn't flinch.

"You focus on your exam," he said. "Let me handle the rest."

At first, I tried to study alone. But after a full week, I had only gotten through a single chapter. Then, almost by chance, I stumbled on a Facebook group for students preparing for the NAPLEX. Some students who had already passed were offering to share access to an expensive online course; one I never could have afforded on my own. I managed to secure a three-month login. It was a turning point. The videos were clear and structured. I began to learn. I began to understand. And slowly, I began to believe.

Diaa would wake up in the morning and find me at the kitchen table, earphones in, eyes locked on the screen. He'd come home after a long shift and find me in the exact same spot. He never made me feel guilty. He kept snacks stocked, reminded me to drink water, and when I pushed myself too far, he'd brush my hair away from my face and say, "You need to let your brain breathe. Just ten minutes of sun."

I rarely listened. But I heard the love in his voice.

"I'm proud of you no matter what happens," he reminded me often. "Just doing this, pushing this hard, that's already a win."

After six weeks of relentless studying, I took a full-length practice exam. The results were clear: I wasn't ready. Panic tried to take over, but there was no time to collapse. Work had become short-staffed. So, I rescheduled.

The new date was December 26th. The day after Christmas.

From the moment I woke up, my body was flooded with panic. My heart pounded so loudly I could hear it in my ears. When the exam began, I moved too slowly, reading questions two, sometimes three times, double-checking every calculation. Time slipped through my fingers. Six hours. That's what I had. And when those hours were up, I still had fifty questions left unanswered.

I left the testing center devastated. When the results came in, I had missed the passing score by fifteen points.

But that number gave me something unexpected: hope. Fifteen points wasn't a failure. It was unfinished business. Had I managed my time, had I reached those final fifty questions, I might have passed.

I waited out the mandatory period, then registered again immediately. My new date was March 9, 2019. I took every remaining vacation day and more unpaid time, three full weeks of nothing but studying.

This time, I was smarter. I trained like a fighter stepping back into the ring.

I printed out a picture of my dream car and taped it above my desk. That was my promise to myself: when you pass, when you become a licensed pharmacist, you're buying that car. Not as a reward. As a symbol. Proof that I rebuilt my life from nothing and turned pain into power.

So once again, I gave it everything I had.

And this time I wasn't afraid.

Chapter 20: When He Carried Me

Becoming a licensed pharmacist meant everything to me. But it also came with something I hadn't fully prepared for: a dramatic shift in my financial standing. Suddenly, I was set to make almost three times more than Diaa.

Diaa and I had always maintained a quiet, respectful understanding about money. We split major expenses, rent, utilities, groceries. For smaller everyday things, we each picked up what we needed. There was no tallying, no tension, just flow.

But I could feel the world watching. Whispers and opinions started to creep in: "Are you sure things won't change now that you're the breadwinner?" "Will you start talking down to him like most women do when they make more?"

Those comments stung ,not because they held truth, but because they reflected other people's fears, not mine. Diaa never gave me a reason to doubt him. He didn't shrink in the face of my success. He celebrated it. He made space for it. He wore my victories like they were his own.

And I, in turn, never let pride get in the way of our partnership. Money didn't make me more valuable; I had always been valuable. And Diaa never measured my worth in earnings, just as I never measured his in checks.

Love isn't a ledger. It's a commitment. And ours remained unshaken.

By June, I had finally finished all the requirements the exams, the intern hours, the paperwork, everything. All that was left was to mail the final form to the Texas Board of Pharmacy and wait for my license to be issued.

I remember standing at the post office counter, sealing the envelope with hands that trembled, not from fear this time, but from disbelief. After everything I had been through, I was here. It was done.

As I walked out into the heat of a Texas summer afternoon, the pavement outside was slick with condensation. I stepped down, and in an instant, I slipped. It happened so fast. I caught myself, sprang up, looked around to make sure no one had seen. I laughed it off. I went home.

But by morning, I was in agony. I couldn't walk. The pain was so intense I couldn't even stand. I had to crawl on my hands and knees just to get to the bathroom.

Diaa had to open the store that morning, and I could see the guilt in his eyes. He held my hand and said, "I'll be back as fast as I can, I promise." He kissed my forehead, tucked a pillow behind my back, and left. It felt like he had just walked out the door when he returned - out of breath, still in his work clothes. He helped me get dressed, gently lifting me as though I were made of glass. He carried me downstairs, one arm beneath my legs, the other around my shoulders, whispering, "I've got you."

No broken bones, just severe muscle trauma and a $2,500 bill. A warning to rest. But of course, I didn't have time to rest. I had a license to receive. A life to build. Children to support.

By mid-July, I was officially promoted to pharmacist. I remember staring at my first paycheck in disbelief, not because of the number I brought home, but because of the deductions. My biweekly taxes and benefit contributions alone were more than I used to make entirely as a pharmacy technician. It was surreal.

With the promotion came more responsibility. My employer wanted me licensed in multiple states, so I got to work ,scheduling licensure exams every two weeks, each new license a stamp of achievement. By the end of 2019, I had earned nine pharmacy licenses.

After all that hard work, all that self-sacrifice, I wanted to do something just for me. So, I did. I decided to get liposuction surgery, a choice made not from vanity, but from a desire to reclaim my body, to feel good in my skin again after carrying so much trauma inside it for so long.

I was bedridden for two full weeks. During those two weeks, Diaa never left my side. He stayed with me at my parents' house, tending to me like I was the most precious thing he had ever held. He changed my dressings, no matter how gory or soaked. He held the urinal beneath me so I could relieve myself. He helped me get dressed. He fed me with his own hands. Not once did he flinch or pull away. His love didn't waver when things got messy and it deepened.

My mother, too, was extraordinary. She brought meals to my bedside three times a day, never repeating a dish. Her care was quiet but steady, like the background music of comfort I hadn't realized I'd missed. For the first time, I felt nurtured by both a man and a mother.

I once thought I had only known the worst of men. I was wrong. Diaa was proof that love could be different. His kindness, his tenderness, his unwavering worry overwhelmed me in the most beautiful way. I felt cherished.

What I didn't know at the time, what I couldn't have imagined- was that just a few years later, I would be doing all of this for him.

Even though I made nearly three times his salary, Diaa refused to lessen his contribution to our shared life. He became even more insistent on paying his share, because, in his words, "A man shouldn't take money from his wife."

He was modest to the core. He rarely shopped for clothes. He never compared himself to others and never let material things define his worth. He adored his old 2002 Mustang, the paint, the seats, and most of all the engine that still roared like a promise. I offered more than once to help him buy a new one, even suggested we finance it together, but he always refused.

"It's not about the car," he said. "It's about living within your means. If I can't afford it, I don't need it."

No credit cards. No loans. No financing. That was his law. He never asked how much I made. Never pried into my savings or questioned how I spent my money. And when I tried to give him expensive gifts, he resisted, so much so that I often had to fight with him just to treat him. His pride wasn't toxic. it was sacred. It wasn't about power or ego. It was about dignity. Self-respect. Principles.

He would buy gifts for my children before I even had the chance. If their phones broke, he replaced them, new screen protectors, new cases, carefully packaged and delivered to Jordan. He never made a show of it. He did it because he loved them. Because they were mine, and that was enough.

When his illness progressed and he couldn't work anymore, he was devastated, not because he lost a job, but because he couldn't contribute. He apologized constantly, his voice full of shame I never once asked him to carry.

And then, quietly, without telling me, he sold the thing he loved most: his Mustang. The car he called his baby. I had begged him not to, told him it would be a collectible one day, the way he kept it in pristine condition. But he sold it anyway. And he gave me almost the entire amount, saving only a few hundred dollars for his daughters.

That was Diaa.

He wanted nothing material from me. He didn't want me to cook or clean or earn or give. He didn't want me for my body or what I could provide. He just wanted me, my love, my companionship. I was his home. His heaven. And he was mine.

He wanted a sofa big enough for both of us so we could snuggle more. That's the kind of love we had, measured not in grand gestures, but in proximity, in warmth, in holding each other close as often as we could.

Now that he's gone, I am lost in ways I cannot begin to explain.

And in the end, I couldn't even hug him.

Cancer was everywhere. It had eaten through his bones, his body, his strength. He was in unbearable pain, and still he tried to protect me, apologizing for needing help, insisting I sleep longer, even trying to manage on his own.

When he was discharged from the hospital for the last time after his surgery, he was heavily medicated for pain management. I shared my fear of addiction, that his pain medication was triggering for me, and that I was scared of him becoming dependent. He stopped taking them. Just like that. No arguments. No blame. Cold turkey. Even as the cancer burned through him, he tried to soothe my wounds. Until he couldn't.

That's the man I lost.

Two men left a mark on my life.

One enslaved me with the very love I gave him using it to break me down until there was almost nothing left.

The other took that ghost of a woman, gathered every shattered piece, and held them with reverence. He nourished me. He loved me like I was a rare diamond, unlike any other.

And then, just as I began to shine again, he was taken from me.

Chapter 21: Between Love and Grief

I've been avoiding this part of the story.

Some pain is too sacred to put into words.

But it's time.

One year and four months have passed since I lost you. And still, when I look in the mirror, I see a woman who looks like me , same eyes, same lips, same voice. The world smiles back at her as if nothing has changed. But behind that familiar face lives someone else entirely. Someone who was split wide open and has been quietly trying to hold the pieces together ever since.

I wear this mask, so others feel comfortable around me. It's easier to hide the hollow ache, to nod and smile and show up to life. But inside, I am still screaming. Still searching for the breath, I lost the day you took your last.

I read something once: "We both died that day, only you stopped breathing. My body kept moving, going through the motions. But my soul? It cracked open."

That is exactly how it feels. I smile. I work. I speak. But I am not the same woman. The world may see something that looks like healing. What they don't see is the part of me that was buried with you.

What they also don't see , what almost no one knew was that while I was losing you, I was also losing everything else at the same time. Your health. My immigration case. My children's future. A lawyer who failed me at the worst possible moment. A system that moved slowly while our lives burned fast.

I was carrying all of it. Every single day. And I carried most of it alone, because you needed me strong, and I refused to let you see me break.

Life had just begun to bloom again.

After we got married and moved in together, everything fell into place so naturally. We created a rhythm date nights, long conversations, your hand always reaching for mine. Whether we were out with friends or just the two of us curled on the couch, I felt like the luckiest woman in the world.

You were the key. I was the lock. Or maybe I was the storm, and you were the calm. We fit imperfectly - perfectly. You, the structured, detail-driven perfectionist. Me, softer, more chaotic, but grounded by your love.

Our home was always immaculate, not because we were trying to impress anyone, but because it was our sanctuary. A sacred space of laughter, music, dancing in the kitchen, and sharing coffee on quiet mornings. We were in sync. You never had to wait for me. I never had to wait for you.

You made everything easier with your dry, sarcastic sense of humor. People lit up when you walked into a room. No outing was ever quite as fun without you. You weren't just my husband. You were my peace. My anchor. My proof that love , the real kind, could exist after all I'd been through.

The only ache that lingered was the absence of my children. But we talked about them constantly, dreaming about the day when they would finally join us. Six kids between us, we laughed about needing a bigger car and bigger pots to feed them all. But we weren't afraid. Not of the future. Not of anything. Because we had each other.

Then came 2020. The world shut down. COVID-19 changed everything, for everyone, except those of us in healthcare. You stayed home. I went to work. But somehow, we found magic in madness.

We walked together every evening, listening to music. I'd dance in public, wild and free, and you'd shake your head, blushing, laughing, pretending to be embarrassed but secretly loving every second. When the gyms closed, we turned our home into a workout space. Your discipline was unmatched. You were proud of your body, and you were pushing me to live a more active and healthier life. After all, we wanted to grow old together; we wanted to be the eighty-year-old couple who dance together regardless of their age or what anyone thinks.

By 2021, we were ready for a new beginning. I was making good living wages as a pharmacist and everyone around us was benefiting from record low interest rates. We started house hunting and stumbled upon a miracle, our dream home, already under construction, suddenly available when the original buyer backed out. We claimed it. It felt like the universe had finally turned in our favor.

We filmed everything, the empty rooms, the plans, the excitement and sent them to the kids. It felt like hope was finally tangible. Like happiness had a heartbeat.

Then the winter storm came. The Texas freeze of 2021. The power that went out our apartment was like an icebox, but you wouldn't let me start the day without my coffee. You lit your welding torch in the cold and heated water just for me.

Who does that? Who thinks of a simple cup of coffee as an act of love that needs to be protected?

You did.

That's the kind of love we had. Steady. Fierce. Unspoken in grand gestures, but alive in every small one. Even frozen mornings couldn't shake us. You were my warmth. You were my home.

The memory of you standing in that dark apartment, shielding me from the cold, will stay with me forever. We ended up at my parents' house with your daughters, because they still had power and a fireplace. I remember how you'd take me on long drives just to warm me up. I was shivering so hard I thought I'd cry from the cold. You saw that before I said a word.

We were the couple, our bond so natural that it looked curated. We furnished our home together, piece by piece, and everyone assumed we had hired an interior designer. But it was simply you, with your perfect eye for balance and comfort, and a little sprinkle of me.

Yes, we had our struggles, especially with immigration, and I'll talk about those later. But we had so many plans. We were finally building a life full of joy. We started planning vacations. Our first trip was for your birthday, a long road trip to Florida to visit your childhood friend. The next year, we celebrated my birthday in Las Vegas with my parents. My father was legally blind, worn down by years of illness, unable to walk for more than five minutes at a time. When he looked around at the noise and the crowds and said, "Just leave me in the lobby and go enjoy your time," you looked at him and said, "How can I enjoy anything without you?" You rented a wheelchair on the spot and pushed my heavy, aching father through the buzzing streets of Vegas for four straight days. We walked nearly 28,000 steps a day. Not once did you complain. Not once did you ask for rest. You were beaming, not because Vegas was fun, but because you made my father happy.

You didn't just become his son. You became the best son anyone could ever hope for. I could speak for days about the things you did for my parents, quiet acts of love that you never asked to be thanked for. You just gave, and gave, and gave.

My asylum was denied in April of 2022, and I was devastated. I searched for a new lawyer with more experience in asylum cases. Since all courts had just reopened after

COVID, most lawyers were not taking new clients, so I looked for someone with five-star ratings and found one M.C I went to her believing she had my best interest at heart.

She agreed to represent me in immigration court for asylum. The other option- dismissing the case- would have left me in limbo. It was $9,500 ++ to represent me in front of immigration court, and another $9,500 ++ to help me get an immigrant visa through my employer, who didn't hesitate to support me.

Wanting to be proactive I explained your full immigration situation to her, including that your daughter/my stepdaughter was a U.S. citizen turning twenty-one in February of 2023 and how we have been together since 2018 married in a religious ceremony only. She charged $500 to obtain the document proving you had entered the United States legally at the port of entry, and we gathered everything we needed so that when Si.K turned twenty-one, we were ready to submit the application the day after her birthday. Not once did she mention that as my stepdaughter, Si.K could have petitioned for me directly, an option that had existed all along, that she, as my lawyer, should have known.

I remember getting a white dress, we took the day off work to get married again. You told me how your boss laughed when you said you were taking the day off to marry me again. He asked you: "How many times will you marry her?" You said, "I will marry her as many times as I can and as many times as it takes."

We read our vows and went for a burger at Red Robin—my favorite, then in my white dress and your sharp suit we went to Home Depot to get supplies for our home. It was August of 2022.

Then came February 2023. Your daughter S.K turned twenty-one. A U.S. citizen, she could finally petition for your green card. After fourteen long years of waiting, you could finally hope to see your family again. Your mother. Your siblings. A life frozen in time, waiting for your return.

We celebrated her birthday and had a wonderful time together, we laughed and danced, full of hope for what was coming.

The day after her birthday is burned in my memory, you held the envelope with both hands before we mailed it, as if it were sacred. Right after we left the post office, you looked at me and asked, "Do you think I'll get my green card without obstacles?"

I laughed. "You waited fourteen years just to send this application. I think that's enough of an obstacle."

We both laughed. Then we had lunch together, hopeful. At peace.

We had one more happy moment before life turned upside down. It was in March 2023, my birthday month. I somehow managed to get tickets to see New Kids on the Block. My teenage heart couldn't believe it, I had their posters covering my bedroom walls, and now I could see them in person. You came with me to that concert and I felt young and alive and safe in your arms.

Life felt perfect. We were planning your fiftieth birthday - California, maybe, or Colorado. But to be honest, the best moments weren't the concerts or the trips. They were when we sat beside each other, scrolling on our phones in silence. No words. Just presence. Your nearness was enough. We didn't need noise to feel full.

Then April 2023 came, and with it, everything shattered.

You had complained about back pain for years, always attributing it to an uncomfortable mattress, or working out too hard, or fixing one of our cars. It had come and gone. But recently it was persistent and worse, and when you went to have it checked, they always sent you home with a prescription for antibiotics and a diagnosis of urinary tract infection, which you were told you would have frequently due to a diverticulum in your bladder. So, you took your medication, and life went on as usual.

I was running late to work, which almost never happened. Halfway there, you called me and asked, "Did you see the photo?"

Confused, I opened my phone and froze. The picture was of the toilet. Filled with blood.

You said quietly, "That was my pee."

I didn't ask any more questions. I turned the car around, called work, and told them I wasn't coming in. This wasn't a UTI. Your primary doctor had said it was just an infection. But I knew. Deep in my bones, I knew this was more than that.

I rushed home. You looked pale, tired, like something inside you had dimmed. Without wasting a second, I drove you to the nearest emergency room.

They rushed you in for imaging. But after the first scan, the doctor came back and said, "There's too much blood, we can't even see the bladder." They started bladder washes, multiple rounds, trying to clear the view. Finally, after what felt like hours, they repeated the scan. The doctor's face told me everything before his mouth did.

"There's something there… we're not sure what it is."

I left the room and collapsed in the hallway. Right there on the cold hospital floor, I broke. I couldn't breathe. The tears came from a place deeper than fear, it was like my soul knew before the diagnosis ever came.

A nurse followed me out. Her eyes were misted with tears. She looked down at me and said softly, "You have a good man in there." I looked up, dazed, and she continued, "His first question was, 'Will I live long enough to bring her girls?'

I felt the world tilt again. Even in his fear, his first thought was of me and my daughters. Even in pain, his love never hesitated.

I begged them to admit him, to keep him for more tests. But they refused. Instead, they handed us referral papers for local urologists. Just like that. Like this was something routine.

The nurse whispered to me, "Call them all. Make as many appointments as you can. It's easier to cancel than to get in." I was fuming. We followed her advice. The first appointment was useless. The second finally moved forward. The doctor scheduled a cystoscopy, but we had to wait two whole weeks for the bleeding to subside.

We returned to the clinic mid-April, trying to convince ourselves it might be a stone. Something fixable. Something small.

As I stepped out to use the restroom, the doctor called me back into the room. You were sitting pale and silent, your hands clenched in your lap. You looked up and said only two words: "No good."

The doctor cleared his throat and said, "It's not what I was hoping for. He's too young... but it's cancer."

I heard the words but couldn't absorb them. Cancer. He was referring you to MD Anderson. He told us it was treatable. That chemotherapy and bladder washes could manage it. That it was "common." That it was "not the worst kind." But I wasn't reassured.

It was around this same time, in the middle of the terror of your diagnosis, that the second blow came. We were trying to sort out my immigration paperwork, my green card, the girls' petitions and someone directed us to a small notary office nearby. A young woman looked over our documents with a kind of casual puzzlement and said, "Why didn't his daughter petition for you? As a stepmother, if you were with him before she turned eighteen, you're treated like a biological parent."

I froze.

You were sitting right beside me. Already sick. Already carrying the weight of a diagnosis, we didn't yet fully understand. And in that small office, we both learned that a door had existed, a door that could have changed everything and that it had been quietly closed without our knowledge.

The marriage certificate my lawyer had told us to obtain the one we got in August of 2022, the day we read our vows and went to Red Robin in my white dress and your sharp suit, that piece of paper had made us appear married after S.K turned twenty. Which meant the petition was complicated. Which meant the window had narrowed.

You were devastated. And you were in anguish. We didn't know the stage of the cancer yet. We were already drowning, and now this.

I confronted my lawyer. Instead of remorse, she met me with indifference. She shrugged and said, "Marriage is very difficult to prove." As if the problem were me.

I cried, raw and helpless, and asked her: "Did you ever ask me for proof, and I failed to provide it? I have thousands of pieces of evidence. You never told me this was even an option. You took it away from me."

She didn't apologize. Not even a flicker of regret. She said coldly that she could file the petition, but it would be up to the interviewing officer.

I understood what that meant. And after you were gone, the officer denied the petition. The chance that should have been mine from the beginning was lost. Not because I didn't qualify. Not because I lacked evidence. But because the person I trusted to guide me failed me when it mattered most.

But I didn't have time to collapse. Because you needed me. And when someone you love is fighting for his life, everything else falls silent.

After everything I had survived, the years of abuse, the escape, the ocean I crossed alone, the sofa I slept on, the exams I passed on no sleep and borrowed money, the life I rebuilt from nothing, after all of that, why was this happening? Why was the one good thing, the one man who had loved me without condition or cruelty, why was he the one being taken?

I had rebuilt my faith slowly, carefully, the way you rebuild anything that has been destroyed. And now I found myself in another crisis, not of grief, but of meaning. Of justice. Of a God I was no longer sure was listening.

Diaa had once told me, in a different dark time: "Whatever brings you peace, follow it."

I was trying. I am still trying. But in those months, peace felt like something that happened to other people. Something I had been permitted to taste briefly, just long enough to know what I was losing.

We had no insurance at first. But I was ready to sell my soul if that's what it took. Before anything else, I contacted immigration. I needed your paperwork expedited. I sent your initial diagnosis and the referral to MD Anderson directly to USCIS. I was calling every hospital, fighting for appointments. Most were booked thirty to forty-five days out. I screamed. I cried. I negotiated. I begged. Eventually, I got you seen sooner.

I went into survival mode. Mama bear mode. I handled everything, the green card, the insurance, the appointments, the research. I read everything about bladder cancer. Every article. Every study. Every treatment guideline. I learned about stages, grades, surgical options, chemotherapy protocols, immunotherapies. I memorized survival rates and case studies. But the more I read, the more my stomach twisted. My gut told me this wasn't an early stage. And my gut has never lied to me.

At that time, my parents were visiting my sister in Egypt. We didn't tell them the full truth , only that you were sick. We didn't want to worry them. We still hoped this would pass.

Then, just one week later, your green card arrived. The same card you had waited fourteen years for.

You held it in your hand like it was a cruel joke. Tears ran down your face. And you said, "What am I supposed to do with this now? I waited all these years just to go home and see my mother… and now I can't go anywhere. I can't let her see me like this."

We held each other and cried. So many dreams… shattered in an instant.

Everyone stepped in. Your boss Kris and his wife Kay moved mountains. He fought for you as if you were family, getting you the best health insurance plan possible, something I could never have imagined securing on my own. I would have sold everything I owned to make sure you received the care you deserved. And I meant it. I would have walked through fire for you.

Zozo and Alex stood with us through every moment. Every scan. Every biopsy. Every terrifying wait for results. They never let us face any of it alone. Their presence was a lifeline in a world that was crumbling under our feet.

I was always the first to see everything, lab results, preliminary scans, radiology reports long before any doctor walked into the room. I saw the numbers, the markers, the shifts in enzymes, the rising flags that only someone in medicine would notice. I saw the shadows that weren't there before. The words like "suspicious" and "concerning." The measurements that told a story no one else had read yet.

And I understood. That was the curse of it. To know too much. To connect the dots before anyone said them aloud. To feel the truth landing in my chest while the room around me was still quiet. Yet every time I opened a new result, I prayed desperately that I was wrong. But they did mean what I knew they meant. And carrying that knowledge alone was one of the heaviest burdens of my life.

Your journey toward a final diagnosis was not just painful, it was brutal. At first, we were told that because you were young, it was likely something localized. Bladder cancer, yes, but treatable. BCG washes. Bladder installations. Routine, almost. Then came another scan. The tone shifted. It might be Stage 2 or 3. Still, no lymph node involvement. We needed an MRI, PET scan, and biopsy.

We did it all. The MRI and PET scans came back no lymph node involvement, tumor markers all negative, no signs of metastasis. I let myself breathe. The window was still open. We had options. Chemo, then surgery, then maybe immunotherapy. It was a hard road, but a road, nonetheless.

And while we waited, I didn't sit still. I buried myself in research. I read everything, medical journals, clinical trials, survivor forums. I learned about bladder cancer staging, grades, progression, and experimental therapies. I found hope in herbs Turkey Tail mushroom, Fucoidan, anything with a shred of evidence. I made sure you took them daily while we waited.

Then came the biopsy. And the doctor walked into the room with a grin. Not the comforting kind. The kind that makes your blood run cold.

He looked at us and said, "It's bad news."

You had locally advanced Stage 4, high-grade bladder cancer. Inoperable. The five-year survival rate was 8%.

The world just stopped. We were negotiating between partial and full bladder removal, and now it wasn't even an option. How do you go from maybe a small surgery to: you can't be saved?

I begged for another opinion. The doctor referred us to Dr. S. L, one of the top urologic surgeons in the country. By some miracle, we got an appointment the following week.

I was prepared. I read every article Dr S.L had published. Every trial he participated in. I studied treatment plans, outcomes, immune therapies, everything.

And when we met him, he changed everything. He looked at you and said: "Why are you so pale, young man? Here's what we're going to do: you'll take chemotherapy, the tumor will shrink, we'll make you a new bladder, we'll give you immunotherapy, and you'll live long enough to become an old man."

That was all we needed. A sliver of hope. We clung to it like oxygen.

In that spirit of hope, we celebrated your fiftieth birthday, surrounded by close friends and family. It was supposed to be a surprise, but you saw all the preparations through the Ring camera. You laughed as you entered the house to one of your favorite songs: "Hey shorty, it's your birthday..."

Everyone who truly loved you was in that room. You could feel it, the warmth, the quiet devotion, the way every eye softened when they looked at you. And somehow, even with the illness living inside you, trying to steal you piece by piece, your humor and your spirit filled the space so completely that the disease seemed powerless.

When you laughed, the cancer disappeared. When you spoke, the room came alive. When you smiled, you forgot there was anything wrong at all. In that room, surrounded by the people who loved you most, you were still the brightest light. And you blew out your fifty birthday candles.

The chemotherapy journey was about to begin, and I threw myself into preparing the only way I knew how, with love disguised as action.

I went to the market and bought every kind of fruit I could find. I washed them carefully, cut them into bite-sized pieces, and packed them into neat containers. I knew you would eat them this way, small, easy, gentle on your stomach.

It was one of the few things I could control in a world suddenly spinning too fast.

I ordered Turkey tail mushrooms and spent hours preparing a proper tincture extract, making sure you received the purest form with real medicinal properties. I researched every step, every temperature, every ratio, as if precision could protect you. I ordered fucoidan, extracted from brown seaweed grown in Japan.

The doctors didn't dismiss any of it. They were surprisingly supportive of whatever herbal remedies you wanted to try, just not on chemo days. They understood what I was trying to do, to give you every possible chance, to fight with every tool available, to love you in all the ways medicine couldn't.

But you, being you, kept forgetting to take them. So, I covered the house with sticky notes. On the fridge door. The mirrors. The doors. Even the toilet. "Drink your fucoidan."

You have been gone for one year and four months now. And that one sticky note, the one on the wall facing the toilet is still there. It survived. That tiny, insignificant piece of paper is still there, looking back at me, reminding me that you are gone. While it remained.

That sticky note sent me into a spiral just a few days ago. Because how is it possible that it remained… and you didn't?

You started Dense Dose MVAC- a chemotherapy regimen so intense and unforgiving, it's known to break even the strongest patients. Administered every two weeks instead of three, it delivers more chemo in less time, giving the body almost no room to recover, but also giving cancer cells no chance to proliferate. Most patients can't tolerate more than four rounds before the side effects become too much. Many stop midway. Many are forced to.

Your first dose was given as an inpatient because you didn't yet have a port. They installed it a week before the second dose. And on the same day you had the surgery for your port placement, my car broke down in the middle of nowhere. I was driving back from El Campo when the car started to malfunction and I had to pull onto a side road, away from the eighteen-wheelers on the highway.

I had asked to leave work early because I couldn't be with you during the procedure. I was trying to get back to you. And even though you had just had surgery that morning, you came to my rescue. You wouldn't leave me stranded. Nothing would stop you. Not even surgery. That was you. Always showing up. Always my hero.

Then there were five more rounds to go. You pushed through six full rounds of DD MVAC. No skipped treatments. No dose adjustments. No complaints. It was one of the hardest regimens available, and you met it head-on like the warrior you were.

Most people never even knew you were sick. Why? Because you had always been bald, that was your signature long before cancer entered our lives. So, when the chemo took what little hair you had, no one noticed a thing. You looked the same. You carried yourself with the same quiet strength, the same dry humor, the same sparkle in your eyes. People were often shocked when they found out. "He has cancer. Really?" They couldn't believe it, because you looked so alive.

What they didn't see was the battle raging beneath the surface. The spreadsheets I made to track every pre-medication. The hours of fruit and vegetable preparation. Some say people stop chemo because of the side effects. But you endured. Maybe it was the herbs. Maybe it was the endless supply of fruits and vegetables I made you eat. Maybe it was only you being you. Superman. You were more than strong. You were superhuman. You made surviving look effortless, because you didn't want cancer to change who you were. And in that defiance, in that grace, you gave all of us strength.

During every infusion, I was the watchful mama bear spreadsheets in hand, making sure no nurse skipped a single pre-medication step. And after six, seven, sometimes eight hours of chemo, we'd go to Ranoish, our favorite little coffee shop. The hookah was great. The food was comforting. It became our post-treatment ritual. Then we'd go home. You'd stay active until the fatigue hit. Then you'd sleep for a couple of days. By the third day, you'd get up, put on your clothes, and head back to work like nothing happened.

After three rounds, you had follow-up scans. And the results?

A miracle.

Dr. Y walked into the room smiling from ear to ear. He said, "I can't stop smiling. My jaw dropped when I looked at the scans." The tumors were almost gone. Only a few abnormal cells remained. You were eligible for surgery. Just like Dr. S.L promised.

We finally dared to believe again.

We held hands in that waiting room and laughed, the kind of laughter that comes after you've been holding your breath for months. We made plans. We talked about California for your fiftieth. We talked about the girls coming. We talked about growing old.

We didn't know then what I know now.

We didn't know that hope, for us, had an expiration date.

Chapter 22: The Invisible Pain

The surgery was set for October 25th, 2023. We were anxious, yes, but also hopeful. Finally, it felt like the nightmare was almost over.

In the days before, we prepared the way you prepare for something you believe will lead to healing. We watched videos of people who had gone through the same surgery, people who were five years out, living full, healthy lives. We took notes. We followed their recommendations. We adjusted our lives accordingly.

I bought a new bed with an adjustable base so you could sit up easily when I wasn't home , something small but thoughtful, a way to give you comfort and independence during recovery. I wanted everything to be perfect for your return. I believed there would be a return worth preparing for.

You were young, strong, and otherwise healthy. That, we believed, was our advantage. That, we believed, would be enough.

We arrived at the hospital at five in the morning, still wrapped in the darkness of early morning. Mom, Zozo, and Alex were with us. Dr. S.L came to speak with us before you were taken in, calm, confident, giving us a reassuring thumbs-up. Then they wheeled you away, and we were sent to the waiting room.

We waited for hours.

S.K came and sat with me for a while, offering quiet company. But eventually, one by one, everyone had to leave. Still, I stayed. I couldn't go anywhere else, not when you were still on that table.

Throughout the day I received updates. Each one was a lifeline. By eight in the evening, the waiting room was closed, and I was asked to leave. But I lingered nearby, not ready to go too far.

Finally, around nine-thirty, Dr. S. L came to find me. He looked calm and smiled. The surgery was successful, he said. Clean margins. No lymph node involvement.

Relief flooded my body. It was over. You had made it through.

When I finally saw you, you were groggy but in good spirits. Even through the haze of anesthesia, your morale was high. You smiled at me, and I clung to that smile like a promise.

The next morning, Dr. S.L came again to reassure us. Everything had gone exactly as planned.

The expected stay was five days. It stretched into two weeks.

The pain wasn't easing. You still hadn't passed gas something that was expected by then. Part of the problem was your deep sense of modesty. You wouldn't allow yourself to pass gas around anyone, and there was always someone in the room. You were trying so hard to stay composed, even in your suffering. But the pain kept building until it became unbearable. Eventually they had to insert a gastric tube through your nose to relieve the trapped gas. It was the only way to ease the pressure.

I moved into the hospital. I slept there, ate there, and lived there. Each morning, I left at six to go to work and returned by nine-thirty every night, exhausted but desperate to be by your side. Alex and Zozo came through, bringing me clean clothes, doing laundry, going to the house every day to feed the fish, sometimes making the trip two or three times in a single day.

After two weeks, the hospital discharged us. It felt rushed since your pain didn't ease. We arrived home around nine in the evening, both of us completely spent. We collapsed into bed.

By seven the next morning, you couldn't take it anymore. You were moaning, your face pale and drenched in sweat.

"Call 911," you said.

An ambulance came and took you back. We spent all day in the ER waiting for a bed. When we were finally transferred to a floor, it was clear no one there knew your history. Not a single note from your surgery team. No context. No understanding of the complexity of your case.

So, I stepped in. I became your nurse, your advocate, your voice. I pushed for us to be transferred back to the surgical floor where at least they knew your name and your story.

The next morning, we were moved. This time we were placed in isolation. You had developed a MRSA infection, a hospital-acquired infection, always a risk in major surgery, and now the name behind the unbearable pain.

It was during this admission that the worst moment came.

You were shaking- not a shiver, a violent, uncontrollable tremors that left all of us helpless and terrified. Without speaking, we moved toward you. Me, Alex, Zozo, S.K and Akbar. One held your arm. Another your leg. We wrapped ourselves around you, trying to steady you with the only thing we had left to give: our presence, our touch, our love.

Through it all, your eyes never left mine. Our gazes were locked, unblinking. Nothing else existed , not the hospital room, not the fear, not even the pain. Just the silent conversation between our eyes.

I'm here. I see you. I'm holding on.

There was a pleading in your expression, and I wanted to crawl inside your pain and take it from you. But all I could do was hold you, as if love alone could be stronger than suffering.

Akbar looked at all of us and said softly, "When I get married, I want someone who looks at me the way you two look at each other."

It was a moment suspended in time.

We waited in the ER for hours that night. It wasn't until after ten that we were finally assigned a room. We were led there in silence, clinging to what little hope we had left.

And then nothing. Thirty minutes passed. Not a single nurse. Not a doctor. Not even a basic check-in. You lay there in pain, barely holding on, and I stood there burning with helpless rage.

I went searching for a nurse. When one finally appeared, she rolled in an IV machine that kept malfunctioning, stopping every five minutes. The line was full of air bubbles, nearly two inches long. Akbar and I took turns expelling them, terrified of what they could do.

I asked the nurse about them. She shrugged and said, "It's fine."

I looked her straight in the eyes and said, "I'll make sure the lawyer knows that when my husband dies from an air embolism."

A new, properly functioning machine appeared almost immediately.

You were still using a day urine bag, the small kind, meant for short use. I asked the nurse to switch it to a night bag. I asked again. And again. She never did. By morning, you were soaked in your own urine. They had to cut your clothes off your body to put you into a hospital gown.

I felt broken. Humiliated for you. Furious for both of us.

We stayed five more days in isolation. Then we were discharged again.

Three days later, Alex called me at work. His voice cracked. You were in excruciating pain and none of the medications were helping. He took you to the hospital. I left work like a storm, racing to meet you at the ER.

The rain was relentless, thick sheets blurring the road ahead. Teddy Swims was playing through the speakers his voice cutting straight through my chest with words I was too afraid to say aloud. I turned it up so high just to keep from falling apart behind the wheel.

By the time I arrived, you had already been admitted straight to the twentieth floor. No more ER waiting. Your pain was undeniable.

They said it was constipation. We stayed three days and were discharged.

A few days later the pain returned, severe and relentless. You took an Uber to your primary care doctor because you didn't want to worry me. Your PCP sent you straight to the ER. When I arrived, Kris was already there, he had dropped everything and come to be with you. That was the kind of man he was.

The doctors said you needed physical therapy. You were discharged after a few days and attended PT sessions at a nearby location. But the pain never left. It only grew.

And so, we returned to the ER once more.

This time, they performed an MRI. And then silence. Four long days passed with no updates, no doctors, no explanations. We waited.

On the fifth day, the doctor and his residents finally appeared. They walked in casually, almost as if delivering routine news, and said: "Oh… there's a metastatic tumor in the hip bone. That's what's been causing the pain."

Just like that. Two months of agony explained away as an afterthought.

They started radiation right there in the hospital. But the damage had already been done.

We had gone in on October 25th with the word cure hanging in the air. We left with a new, devastating diagnosis.

And the cruelest part? The bone tumor had been there from the beginning. Visible in the very first scan. While we were celebrating that the bladder tumor was shrinking, the one in his bone was silently growing. It had been missed by MD Anderson, by Baylor, by every scan before and during the surgery, and throughout his entire hospital stay or that was just what they wanted us to believe so we don't hold them responsible.

For two months, we were told it was constipation. Post-surgical healing. Intestinal paralysis. Physical therapy. Everything except the truth.

I knew something was wrong long before they admitted it. I had asked at every morning round: could it be metastatic? Could the cancer have spread to his bones? Every morning, I was brushed off. And every morning, the man I loved suffered through pain that made him tremble, that left him unable to sleep, eat, or move.

When the truth finally came, all they gave us was: "We're sorry."

What are you supposed to do with an apology when your husband has suffered the unimaginable? When you begged them to listen and they dismissed you, over and over, while the cancer spread and the man you love faded before your eyes?

I reached out to malpractice lawyers. Not for money. I wanted someone to be held accountable. I wanted them to hurt the way we had hurt.

The lawyers listened. They shook their heads. They said yes, this was clear neglect, yes, something went very wrong.

And then they said: "There are no damages."

Because he hadn't lost the wrong limb. Because there was no single visible mistake that fit the legal definition. What we had endured, the multiple discharges, the missed diagnosis, the months of agony was considered acceptable.

Not even help with the medical bills. Not even a formal acknowledgment of what had been stolen from us.

My husband was dying. And the system that had failed him simply moved on.

But one thing remained constant through all of it.

Diaa was never alone.

No matter how exhausted we were, no matter how many shifts we had to juggle, we made sure of that. Me, Alex, Zozo, S.K, E.K and Kay. We changed our schedules, took turns, and showed up. Kay became his hospital wife, the name stuck, and we laughed about it even there, even then. Doctors would walk in and address her as the spouse, going over his chart. We'd gently correct them: "I'm his wife," I'd say, smiling through the exhaustion.

Kris would take my hand and say, "Come with me, new wife. Let Kay stay with her hospital husband."

And in that room full of monitors and medications, we found moments to laugh. We found slivers of light. Because Diaa was still Diaa. And we were still surrounded by love.

Even there. Even then.

Chapter 23: The Avalanche

There was a moment, so quiet I almost missed it, when the word cure quietly disappeared from the room.

It had once been everywhere. On the lips of every doctor, between every heartbeat, woven into every sleepless night I survived next to your hospital bed.

Cure. That word held us up, gave us something to fight for. It was our future. Our reward for enduring the unendurable.

But now, it was gone. No one said it aloud, but I felt it. Like a thread slipping silently through my fingers.

And in its place came something colder, more fragile, more terrifying: time. Just time. Time to slow the pain. Time to shrink what they should have seen. Time to be together, even if it meant watching you fade.

Hope didn't leave us. But it changed shape. It became something quieter, more desperate. It became the wish for one more sunrise, one more kiss, one more day where you could smile without flinching.

We no longer fought for a cure. We fought for moments. And I was ready to give everything for just a few more of them.

From that day on, Diaa lived on the wrong side of every statistic. The immunotherapy for bladder cancer once hailed with a 70% response rate failed to keep his tumor under control. Then came a new treatment, just approved by the FDA after twenty years of research. It offered over a 50% response rate, and for some, complete remission for over thirty months. I clung to that number like a lifeline, whispering to Diaa, "This could be it... maybe this one is different."

But it wasn't. That too did nothing. He remained on the losing side of hope.

Even radiation betrayed him. The doctors assured us that 99% of patients feel no pain from radiation. But Diaa my Diaa, was the 1%. The exception. The unlucky one. He endured a pain so sharp, so constant, that I could feel it ripping through both our spirits.

And still, I kept telling him a miracle was coming. "There's always one," I said. "Why not you?" I needed him to believe it. But in truth, I was the one who needed convincing. I wasn't speaking to him, I was pleading with God, with fate, with the universe. Trying to drown out the silence of reality with words full of borrowed hope.

We had a few good days, days where life almost looked normal again. We laughed, cooked, even argued about what to watch on TV. For fleeting moments, I let myself believe we had turned a corner.

But after three months of immunotherapy, the scan shattered that illusion. The cancer had spread to his liver, spine, ribs, and clavicle. Metastases. Not just one, but many. The words felt like daggers, each location another betrayal of our hope.

I became a machine, reading, researching, digging through every treatment ever attempted. I chased options both FDA-approved and still tucked away in medical journals, whispered about in conferences. I found a procedure called stereotactic MRI-guided thermal ablation that could precisely destroy multiple liver metastases in one session. It was cutting-edge, almost miraculous, with early results that sparked real hope. But Diaa's cancer was high-grade, aggressive, and fast-moving and because this treatment was still considered experimental, no insurance would cover it. I fought anyway, calling clinics, emailing doctors, calculating costs, begging the universe to give us just one break.

But hope, too, seemed experimental.

Diaa went through radiation sessions that left him in unimaginable pain. What was supposed to relieve his suffering ended up compounding it. His body burned from the inside out, and the pain medications meant to help brought their own cruel consequences. He was hospitalized multiple times. Constipation from the opioids became unbearable, turning every attempt at comfort into another layer of torment.

Still, I kept trying to find a crack of light in the darkness. "Diaa," I whispered again and again, "you're in Houston , the world's beacon for cancer treatment. If there's any place where a miracle could happen, it's here."

That's when Dr. Y told us about a new clinical trial at MD Anderson. The drug was called Enhertu, a targeted therapy already established for HER2-positive breast cancer. Now researchers were expanding its reach, studying its effects on other solid tumors with the same HER2 3+ profile. Diaa's cancer was an exact match.

For a brief moment, it felt like the universe was offering us a second chance.

Dr. Y acted quickly, connecting us with the MD Anderson team leading the trial. Diaa was still young, and despite everything, we convinced ourselves he was strong enough. We began the enrollment process right away, tedious, full of paperwork, labs, scans but we didn't care. We had hope again. Real, clinical, data-backed hope.

But the disease didn't wait.

His pain became unbearable. His weight began to drop. Almost overnight, he could no longer move the way he used to. His body was giving out, piece by piece.

Then, just as we were nearing the final steps of enrollment, we were told the words we feared most: Diaa no longer qualified. His condition had declined too quickly. He wasn't strong enough.

He turned to the doctor, his voice soft but certain, and asked, "What does that mean?"

And with a gravity that swallowed the room, the doctor replied, "It means… you have a few weeks left."

Diaa looked at the doctor and asked quietly, "Will it be painful?"

He had accepted the idea of death with a calm I couldn't fathom. But what he couldn't bear was the thought of suffering. Pain was the only thing he feared. Not leaving this world, not saying goodbye. Just the pain.

And the truth is, his pain was already excruciating. But not once did he complain. He never said, "Why me?" He never yelled. He was never unkind. Even in the worst of it, he held on to grace. And that made it harder to watch him suffer.

The doctor explained everything gently, as if trying to soften the inevitable. "Your liver will begin to shut down as the tumors grow. As toxins build up, you'll feel more and more fatigued. You'll sleep most of the time. And the pain medications will only add to that drowsiness… Eventually, you'll pass in your sleep."

Diaa nodded, quietly absorbing the reality of it.

But I wasn't ready to let go. Not yet. I asked, almost breathless, "What if we get the new treatment, even if insurance won't cover it? I'll sell the house. I'll find a way to pay. Just give us a chance."

The doctor looked at me with kind eyes, the kind that knew the limits of medicine and the weight of a woman's love.

He said he would try, even though there was less than a 1% chance the insurance would approve it. It was a whisper of possibility in a room full of silence.

That night, at ten p.m., the phone rang. It was Dr. H, who supervised Diaa's enrollment.

"Diaa will get his first infusion in the morning," he said.

I froze. I felt my knees weaken under the weight of that sentence. It didn't feel real, it felt divine. I stood there, holding the phone, shaking, with tears pouring down my face.

This was the miracle. I was sure of it. Because these things don't just happen. Not at the last minute. Not when all doors were supposed to be closed. This wasn't chance. This was God.

And once again, I believed.

But what made it truly unbearable was the cruel similarity between the side effects of the infusion and the doctor's description of dying. Fatigue. Hallucinations. Long stretches of sleep. The doctor had warned us, this is how the body shuts down when the liver begins to fail. But those same symptoms were listed under the treatment side effects we had fought so hard to receive. And so, I lived in a fog of not knowing. Was the drug working? Was he resting? Or was I watching him die, slowly, silently?

I would sit next to him in bed, frozen in that terrible uncertainty. And I did something I never told anyone.

I began to sync my breathing to his.

I would hold my breath and wait just to make sure he took his next one. And when he did, I would exhale with him, matching his rhythm like we were sharing the same fragile thread of life. If he paused too long between breaths, I would panic silently, holding myself completely still, until I saw his chest rise again and I could breathe with him once more.

I wasn't just watching him breathe. I was breathing for him. With him. As if I could carry part of the weight of dying on his behalf.

Some days, he was unresponsive. Other days, he would speak through hallucinations, seeing people and places that weren't there. I didn't know what was real anymore. All I knew was I was losing him, whether to the treatment or to the cancer, I couldn't tell.

I started calling his friends, asking them to come and say goodbye. But I never let anyone cry in front of him. Not even once. I saw people who loved him crumble at his bedside and fall to their knees, their faces red with grief. And I stood between them and his bed like a soldier and said softly, "Please… not here. Don't let him see you break."

Because I couldn't afford to break. Not yet. Inside, I was already shattered. But on the outside, I was still the anchor.

This nightmare lasted for two long weeks. Two weeks of terror of breath-holding, of living between life and death.

And then, suddenly, as if God Himself had touched him, Diaa woke up.

He was alert. He was moving without pain. He was eating again. He was himself again.

It was like watching a man come back from the dead. The moment he opened his eyes and moved without wincing; he started making plans. His voice had purpose again. "I need to change the house lights," he said. "They're too dim." He walked up the stairs without help. He smiled more. He laughed. He started living , not surviving.

I told Dr. H about the sudden improvement, and he was thrilled. He scheduled six more infusions, one every three weeks. It felt like we had stepped off the battlefield and into recovery. The second infusion came a week later, and with it, a fresh set of scans.

The results stunned everyone. Five out of seven lesions in the liver had shrunk. And the bone lesions were starting to heal.

And what better reason to celebrate than Diaa's fifty-first birthday?

It became more than just a birthday it was a triumph, a sacred milestone. Everyone wanted to be there. Love surrounded us like sunlight after a storm.

My mom and dad were coming. My brother and his wife, Zozo and Alex, who had become part of our extended family, made plans to join. His daughters, S.K, E.K, and L.K were all there, each in their own way caring for him with so much love. Wassim and Kristeen, the very first friends Diaa made in the United States, came too. They weren't just friends, they were family, the kind you choose, the kind who show up. And then there were Kris and Kay, another steady source of love who stood by us when the world felt shaky.

The house began to fill with voices, laughter, cooking smells, and soft light. After weeks of sterile hospital rooms and tear-choked silence, this gathering felt like resurrection. Diaa was glowing. He was laughing. He was planning.

It felt like God had paused time for us, just long enough to remind us what joy felt like. We laughed and danced, took videos and pictures to make that day last forever.

Kris and Kay, his boss and his wife were so much more than that. They treated us like family from the very beginning. To Kris, Diaa wasn't just a colleague. He was a big brother. Closer to him than his own twin.

Their bond went far beyond business, it was built on love, loyalty, and a quiet daily rhythm that spoke volumes. Kris had the code to our front door, and it was never a formality, it was part of the routine. On mornings when it was his turn to drop his kids at school, he would come straight to our house. He'd let himself in like family does, make a pot of coffee, and gently wake Diaa. Then the two of them would sit together on sofa smoking hookah, sipping coffee, talking about everything and nothing, just soaking in each other's company before heading off to work. That was their time. Sacred. Consistent. A ritual of connection that anchored them both.

Before Diaa's diagnosis, Kris had decided to open a new jewelry store in First Colony Mall, his most ambitious expansion. He chose Diaa to run it. Everyone referred to it as "Diaa's store," because it was his. He was meant to manage it, lead it, supervise the other kiosks, and shape its success. Kris took him shopping picked out tailored suits and crisp shirts, knowing exactly how Diaa would look in them: polished, sharp, dignified, carrying the quiet authority of a man who owned every room he walked into.

But Diaa never had the chance to wear the new clothes. The suits, the shirts, carefully chosen and full of promise, still hang in the closet. Labels untouched. Sleeves never rolled. Collars never smoothed by his hands. They wait in silence, holding all the plans we made and never got to live.

Now, they stand as more than just fabric. They are monuments to a life interrupted, to a future that was almost within reach. Every time I open that closet, I see not just what he didn't get to wear, but who he was, the man who was bigger than life, who filled every room with warmth, charisma, and quiet strength.

Grief doesn't come in grand moments. It comes in the smallest, most ordinary ones, like reaching for something in the closet and brushing your hand against a sleeve that never got worn.

Those three weeks of laughter and planning felt like a gift. Diaa was energetic, full of life, and the light had returned to his eyes. For a little while, we were allowed to breathe.

But then, as always, reality crept back in.

There was a mix-up with his third infusion appointment. After countless phone calls and back-and-forth with the hospital, we finally got him back on track, but at a different MD Anderson location. We were there by eight in the morning, hopeful and ready. We had back-to-back appointments, but the clinic was severely behind. His infusion, originally scheduled for noon, didn't begin until nearly five in the evening. By mid-afternoon, Diaa was exhausted, his patience worn thin. At one point, he looked at me, his voice flat, and said, "Let's just go home." But we stayed. I gently convinced him to hold on a little longer. We had come so far.

It was a Friday. We finished his infusion around seven in the evening and like we always did it, we chose joy, no matter how small. We went to our regular spot. We ordered our favorite food. We had hookah. We pretended, just for that evening, that it was just a normal Friday night.

Then we went home, holding onto the quiet comfort of routine, not knowing it would be one of the last moments that still felt that simple.

After his third infusion, Diaa was tired and low on energy for a few days which we knew to expect. We gave his body time to recover. I let him rest, encouraged him to eat, and stayed close.

Then came Wednesday.

I woke up to a loud banging on our front door. Confused and startled, I opened it to find USCIS agents standing outside. They were conducting a home visit to verify our marital status. In the middle of everything, cancer, treatment, recovery they showed up demanding proof that our love was real. They took photos. Asked questions. Made their notes. And then, without so much as a word of acknowledgment, they left.

Diaa, exhausted, went back to sleep. I stood there in the quiet afterward, trying to catch my breath. The cruelty of it being questioned about the truth of a love that had already endured so much felt almost unbearable.

A few hours later, he woke up.

And everything had changed.

He was in severe pain sharp, stabbing pain when he breathed. The ease we had seen just days before was gone. I rushed him to the emergency room.

They ran tests, ordered scans, and drew blood. But no one came to talk to us. No doctor. No nurse with answers.

But I had access to his patient portal. And so, I checked. And there it was, staring back at me in cold, clinical language: the tumors were growing back. New metastases were appearing on the bone scan. There was opacity in the lungs, a shadow, a warning sign.

And just like that, it was over.

Hope was taken from us for the last time.

There were no words, no dramatic moments. Just silence, and a screen. A few sterile lines of text that shattered the miracle we thought we had found.

Chapter 24: Heaven Needed an Angel

What now?

I stood there, staring at the screen, my fingers still on the keyboard, as if I could type my way into a different reality. The words were right there metastases, progression, opacity but they didn't make sense. Not after everything. Not after the miracle. Not after the suits still hanging in the closet.

What am I supposed to do now? Do I tell him? Do I wait for the doctor? Do I scream? Do I beg?

I knew I should cry, but I couldn't. I should have run out of that room and found someone, anyone, to give me a different version of this truth. But I knew they would say the same thing, only slower, only colder.

The cancer is back. The miracle is over.

Do I start preparing for goodbye? Do I plan the last days of the love of my life like a to-do list? Do I keep pretending to be strong because everyone expects me to?

I didn't even know how to hold his hand. I didn't want him to see it in my face. I didn't want to be the one who took hope away from him, not again. But inside, I was screaming. Please, God. Not yet. Not like this.

I thought we had time. I thought we had a second chance. I thought I could save him.

But now, I didn't know how to move. I didn't know how to breathe. I only knew that whatever happened next, I'd be walking through hell with a broken heart and pretending I knew the way.

We were taken to the newly upgraded palliative care floor, modern, quiet, with spacious rooms and large windows. It was beautiful in a way that almost felt cruel, as if softness could somehow cushion what was coming.

Once again, I moved back in with him. My place was by his side, as it had always been.

I never left his side during any of his hospital stays. Not for a better bed. Not for a shower at home. Not for a full night's sleep in a room without machines. When he slept in that hospital, that was where I slept in a chair that folded into something narrow and hard, turned always to face him, close enough that my hand could find his in the dark.

And Diaa no matter how much pain he was in, no matter how deep the fog of medication, would reach across his bedside table and move everything aside. His phone. His water. The tissues. Anything that stood between his eyes and my face. He cleared it all away without a word, every single time, in every room, in every hospital, through every admission.

We never discussed it. We never had to. It was simply what we did. A quiet agreement between two people who had decided: as long as we can see each other, we are not yet lost.

I didn't want to miss a single moment, a single breath. I wanted to memorize the rise and fall of his chest, the curve of his fingers, the way his eyelashes moved when he dreamed. And I knew, without ever saying it, that he was doing the same.

We didn't say it out loud. But we both knew this was our goodbye. Not in one sentence. Not in a dramatic moment. But in the way we refused to stop looking at each other. In the way our hands stayed locked through every hour of the night. In the quiet comfort of just being there, in the same space, still tethered together by love, even as his body slipped further away.

I spoke to the attending doctor alone. I needed the truth unfiltered and unsoftened. He told me the new immunotherapy had stopped working. The cancer cells had mutated and evolved past the treatment. There was one last option, one final line of defense but the success rate was barely 20%. And Diaa's liver enzymes were off the charts, too unstable to move forward. They needed to wait until his levels returned to normal before considering anything else. But I already knew we didn't have that kind of time.

I stood there, nodding, listening, holding back the scream rising inside me.

Then I looked the doctor in the eyes and said, "Please. Don't talk about any of this in front of him. I don't want him to feel what I'm feeling."

Because I was drowning. But he didn't need to know that. I couldn't take away the cancer. I couldn't stop his pain. But I could shield him from the despair, the percentages, the growing shadow of goodbye. I would hold this unbearable grief silently in my chest and smile when he opened his eyes, make small jokes while my heart cracked in silence. Because I would protect him for as long as I could.

Every morning, the routine began the same. The nurses would come in early, gently wake him, and draw his blood. Then the waiting would begin the quiet, agonizing wait for results. I sat in that chair beside him, pretending to be calm, but inside I was unraveling.

And while we waited, everyone around us was trying to help. Could we medically evacuate him to Saudi Arabia? It had happened before, flights arranged with full medical staff. We started making calls. Everyone reached out: friends, doctors we barely knew, contacts who might know someone, anyone who could move things faster.

Diaa wanted to go home. He wanted to see his mother. But not like this. He didn't want her last memory of him to be a frail version of the man she raised. He didn't want to arrive in a wheelchair, in pain, as a patient. He wanted to walk in. Smile. Be her son. Whole.

And then there were the girls. He never stopped saying it: "I just want to live long enough to bring her girls."

I had tried once after his surgery, filing for humanitarian parole, pouring in thousands of dollars, waiting months, praying. Denied. His youngest sister applied for a U.S. visa. Twice. I worked with the hospital's social worker, asking for help to get the girls temporary tourist visas, just to come and see him. Even lawyers with decades of experience couldn't make it happen. But I tried anyway. My son applied for expedited visas for his sisters. For a moment, it looked like something might move. But the interview was scheduled for the end of December four months too late.

Another failed attempt.

They decided on a spinal nerve block as a last effort to ease his suffering to give him some quality of life, some ability to reposition, to rest, to breathe without agony. But Diaa remembered the bone biopsy, how it left him shaking, drenched in sweat, traumatized. His anxiety was sky-high, and even the idea of another procedure brought a fear I had never seen in his eyes before. Still, he went through with it.

It took two more weeks to finally get his pain under control. By then, he was physically and emotionally exhausted. So was I.

He was now considered terminal. The goal had shifted no longer to fight the disease, but to make sure he was comfortable while his body slowly surrendered, piece by piece.

They had to tell him. Not just the words I had shielded him from for so long, but the raw, undeniable reality: "You have three months to live, maybe four."

I had no choice, no say in the matter anymore. Doctors were obligated to speak, to plan, to begin the conversations I had been dreading since the day he was diagnosed. We had to talk about end-of-life care. We had to ask where he wanted his final resting place to be.

I was dying on the inside, but I had to stay upright.

He sat there in silence, listening carefully as they delivered the words no one should ever have to hear. There was no anger. No tears. Just the quiet composure of a man who had already known, deep down, what they were about to say. They spoke gently, offering grief counseling and the option of seeing a minister. Then came the question that felt like closing a final door: "Where would you like to spend the rest of your life?"

Diaa said nothing. Not then. Not for a long while. His silence wasn't fearful. It wasn't even shock. It was the silence of a man already halfway between this world and the next, trying to make peace with the time he had left.

And I sat beside him, holding the folder in my lap, trying not to fall apart under the weight of it all.

Then came the part no one prepares you for, telling the people you love that the person they love is dying.

One of the most emotional visits came from his ex-wife and her family, people he hadn't seen since the separation. For Diaa, it was overwhelming. The emotional weight, the history, the grief all collided in that moment. He had a painful episode while they were there, and I could feel it wasn't just physical; it was anxiety too. But something sacred happened in that room.

His ex-wife asked for his forgiveness. And Diaa, without hesitation, said softly, "I forgave you a long time ago."

Then I turned to her, holding back my own tears, and said, "Please forgive him too. You're the only person he ever hurt in this life."

She nodded; eyes filled with emotion. "I do," she said. "And now I understand why God sent you to him. I could never have taken care of him the way you did. You're so strong. I don't know how you keep a calm face and don't break in front of him."

I didn't answer. There were no words for the kind of strength that comes from love so deep it swallows grief whole just to keep the other person safe from it.

Some friends couldn't bring themselves to come. It was too much, seeing him like that, watching the once vibrant, full-of-life man fade in a hospital bed. Kristeen loved him as a brother, they were so much alike they finished each other sentences and talked as if they shared a brain and I knew that she couldn't hold her tears in front of him, so I understood.

But others came faithfully. Kris and Kay were there every morning before work, steady, unwavering.

Zozo and Alex came almost every day, bringing warmth and quiet support. Wassim visited twice a week when he wasn't working, staying by his side, just being present.

We were surrounded by love. And still, I felt like I was holding the sky up with my bare hands.

And when we were finally discharged, hospice was already waiting for us at home.

We walked through the door together, Diaa in his wheelchair, me holding back tears and were greeted by hospice nurses and paperwork. It was the third week of September. We were home. But it didn't feel like the homecoming we had imagined. There were no celebrations. No peace. Just the quiet hum of machines and the whispered countdown of time.

At home, Diaa was placed on a carefully managed pain regimen, fentanyl patches, hydromorphone every two hours, and liquid morphine for breakthrough pain. Lorazepam helped with the anxiety and sleep that had both become difficult to manage.

We coordinated our lives around him. Everyone rearranged work schedules so that he would never be alone. We created a rotation, a plan, a structure meant to hold him in love and vigilance.

There were days when S.K was supposed to be caring for him. But exhaustion had taken over, and she slept so deeply that when he needed her, she couldn't hear him. One day, Diaa tried to get his pain medication himself. He was too weak. He fell. And she didn't wake up.

Lying on the floor, helpless, hurting, he called me. His voice was trembling, humiliated, scared. I froze in helpless disbelief and called my mother, begging her to rush to the house and help him.

I will never forget that call. The man who had taken care of everyone, who was proud and dignified even in his suffering, now lay on the ground alone, in pain. We stopped relying on her after that.

You might wonder why my mother wasn't on the care rotation. The truth is, she couldn't be. My father old, nearly blind, fragile in body but not in heart needed her care. She was his eyes, his hands, his stability.

But what most people didn't see was just how much my father loved Diaa. So much so that every time Diaa was admitted to the hospital, my father would have a cardiac episode. Not once. Twice. As if his heart could no longer take the weight of watching Diaa suffer. Even when we were still going through the initial diagnosis and my parents were visiting my sister in Egypt, the very night we told them Diaa might be sick, my father fainted. He hit his head. Collapsed under the weight of the news.

That is how much he loved him.

Diaa brought light with him not the loud kind, but a soft, steady glow that warmed every room he entered. People didn't just love him. They felt better in his presence. And when he was gone, or even hurting, it was as if the light went out.

My family felt that loss even before it came. My mom once said to me, "It's your fault that we are in so much pain. If you hadn't met him and married him, none of us would have known him. And our hearts wouldn't be shattered like this." I understood what they meant. It wasn't blame. It was grief. Diaa didn't just belong to me. He belonged to all of us.

Hospice care became our new rhythm. The nurse came three times a week, monitoring his vitals, adjusting medications, gently guiding us through the unspoken countdown. A nurse's assistant visited twice a week to help with the more personal things, shaving, bathing, small acts that meant everything when your body no longer cooperates.

But Diaa was modest, always had been. He didn't feel comfortable being exposed in front of strangers. So, when it came time for him to shower, he would stay in his boxers, and I would be there every time. I helped him dry off, carefully patting his skin just like he used to when he accused of not knowing how to dry myself after bathing. I helped him put on fresh clothes, smoothed the fabric over his shoulders, dabbed his face with a warm towel. And every single time, I would finish by putting on his signature cologne, a scent that was uniquely him. Warm, clean, comforting, strong.

What amazed me was that he never had body odor, not even after days without a proper shower. His skin always smelled heavenly, as if even in illness, his soul couldn't help but shine through.

These rituals became sacred to me. A final way to care for him. A final way to show love, without words, without fear.

His decline was gradual. We didn't notice it at first — we were with him all the time, too close to the flame to see it dimming. Every day was filled with care, with small victories: eating, sitting outside the bedroom, talking. We clung to those moments like lifelines.

But now, when I look at photos from that time, I can see it, how life was leaving him a tiny bit more each day. The sparkle in his eyes dulled slowly, gently. His smile, still warm, had begun to flicker.

In January, not long after his surgery, he had told me, "I wish we had a deep couch again like the one we had when we first got married. So, we could both fit and snuggle."

So, I sold our sofas. And I bought two deep, soft couches, just like he remembered. When we curled up together on them, he leaned into me, closed his eyes, and whispered, "This snuggle is my heaven."

And all I could think was this is the heaven I'm going to lose.

We watched TV shows together, though he never really liked shows, he did it for me. We watched Bridgerton because it was light and easy to follow. Sometimes he would fall asleep halfway through, his head resting gently against my shoulder. And while he slept, I would look at him, trying to memorize everything, from his legs to his knees, his feet with those long toes we used to laugh about. His hands, the way his fingers curved, how he chewed his nails without thinking. His body, once strong and powerful, now fragile and thin, yet still so beloved.

I traced his beauty marks with my eyes. Studied the length of his eyelashes. I held his hand and tried to savor that feeling the warmth, the weight, the texture, so I wouldn't forget.

Because part of me already knew these were the last pages. And I was trying to memorize the story before the book closed forever.

Those final two months felt like living inside a pendulum. We swung between days that felt almost normal when Diaa was alert, present, with us physically and mentally and days where he drifted far away, lost in a space none of us could enter. On those days, he would sleep most of the time, his breath shallow, his eyes fluttering. And when he did speak, it was to people we couldn't see.

It was as if he existed on another level of consciousness, a space just beyond the veil, and we were not allowed in. We would ask him gently, "Diaa, who are you talking to?"

And true to himself- his sarcasm never left - he'd smirk and say, "I'm not telling you. I'll take that secret to the grave."

And he did. To this day, we never knew who he was speaking to. Angels? Loved ones? God? Or perhaps a piece of himself preparing to let go.

There were moments when we thought we were losing him, when the brain fog became so dense he didn't recognize things or would slip into confusion. But then we would give him the lactulose syrup- thick, sweet, and disgusting, but miraculous in its effect. Lactulose helps rid the brain of ammonia, which builds up when the liver fails. And when it worked, it brought him back to us. Clear-eyed. Sharp-witted. Still Diaa.

We lived for those returns. They were brief, but precious. Like catching glimpses of someone you love in a dream, just long enough to remember how it felt to be fully known.

And just like that, we were back on the roller coaster.

I had my green card interview on October 23rd. It was denied because of my previous lawyer's advice.

But the night before that interview, when everything in me was bracing for another blow, my son called. He told me the girls had suddenly gotten an open slot for a visa interview. It was happening that Thursday.

I told him not to get his hopes up. "It's already paid for," I said. "They might as well go. Just don't expect too much."

But that night, he messaged me: "They got the visa."

I couldn't believe it. After all these years. After all the begging, the letters, the denials. It was approved. It was a miracle. The girls were coming.

I was so overwhelmed I went to wake Diaa, even in his weakened state. I whispered to him through my tears: "The girls are coming."

The next morning, he was mentally clear, present. I told him again, fully this time. "Their flight will be next Friday. I'll book it now."

He looked at me, his eyes soft but certain. "I don't think I'll make it till next Friday."

So, I booked them a flight for the next day. November 2nd.

That was the day I had been dreaming of for eight and a half years, the day I would finally see my daughters again. But it felt like I had been cheated by the universe. Why did it have to be this way? Why did I have to lose my husband to finally see my children? Was it too much to ask for both?

Why couldn't I be allowed to reunite with my daughters without death being the price?

I remember Diaa crying when his green card was approved so quickly because of his diagnosis. He wanted that card so he could travel to see his mother in Saudi Arabia. But by then, it was too late. His pain, his appointments, his treatments all made travel impossible, his happiness was stolen and so was mine.

Sometimes I wonder. What if we had gone to Saudi Arabia from the beginning? What if he had started treatment there instead of here?

I know the United States is considered the world leader in medicine. But in our experience, the system failed him at every turn. In Saudi Arabia or Jordan, he would have been admitted to hospital the same day he walked into the ER. He would have received chemotherapy within the week. Here, it took over two months after diagnosis before he received his first round of treatment.

We lost time. And in cancer, time is everything.

So yes, November 2nd was the day I held my daughters again. But it was also the day he started to let go. life. And in between joy and sorrow, I kept asking one question: why did love have to cost me everything I ever had to gain?

I had one day to prepare for the girls' arrival. I went on a shopping spree, frantic but focused. Blankets, towels, toothbrushes, shampoo, everything I thought they'd need. The truth is, they were never supposed to stay in the U.S. long-term. The plan was for them to visit, maybe stay a few months, and return. But life happened. Death happened. And nothing would ever be the same.

We had a house full of people waiting to welcome them. And I drove to the airport with Alex and Zozo, heart pounding with a mix of joy and dread.

My girls. Walking toward me at the airport, wide-eyed, uncertain, grown. It was emotional- too emotional - and before I could even begin to cry, N.K.S looked at me and said softly, "Don't cry."

So, I didn't. I swallowed the lump in my throat, smiled through my tears, and held them close like I never wanted to let go again.

On the drive home, I checked my phone. There it was the last message I would ever receive from Diaa.

"Where are you now?"

Just that. He was waiting for us. Waiting for me. For them. For one last moment together.

Before the girls had even arrived, I had promised them something simple, something joyful - fireworks. So, when we got home, I stepped outside and set off a single display. It wasn't grand, but it lit the sky in a brief burst of color. A promise kept.

We had dinner. We sat together. And one by one, the visitors went home. And I was left holding the impossible- joy and grief in the same breath, reunited with my daughters while slowly saying goodbye to the love of my life.

I truly believe Diaa fought until the girls arrived. And once they were here, once he knew I wouldn't be alone, he stopped fighting. Something in him softened. Released. He had kept his promise. And now, he could rest.

The next morning, for the first time since we were discharged from the hospital Diaa woke up before all of us. He wanted to take the girls out for breakfast.

I remember exactly what he wore. Loose pants that barely fit from all the weight he had lost. A button-up shirt. And his favorite white Vans sneakers. He looked thin, but glowing. His voice was strong, full of joy, like a man who had just completed something sacred.

We went out to eat, and he even called Wassim to join us. His energy that morning was full of light, present, steady, alive. After breakfast, he asked to stop at a store where one of his friends worked, the friend we borrowed blankets from during Harvy. He wanted to smoke hookah and get tobacco. When his friend saw him, she ran toward him to hug him, but he raised a hand, gently joking, "Easy… you might break me."

I smiled and said, "The girls are outside." She burst into tears and rushed out to meet them.

Then we went to visit my parents and saw my brother there too. It felt like a reunion, simple, beautiful, full of unspoken meaning.

On the drive home, Diaa had one more stop in mind. He wanted to get new fish for his tank. So, he went into the aquarium store with the girls. They picked out fish together, naming them one by one with laughter and love.

And that was the last time Diaa ever left the house.

After that final day out, his decline was swift. It was like his body had been holding on for that one last burst of life and once it had given that, it began to unravel. Quickly. Brutally.

He became a shadow of himself. Every time I looked at him, I was reminded of that scene from Twilight, the one where Bella is pregnant, her body wasting away, every bone pressing against translucent skin. That was my favorite movie. And now I can't watch it anymore, because it reminds me of him.

You could count the vertebrae in his spine, one by one. His ribs jutted out beneath skin that had lost its color, its warmth. Even the whites of his eyes had changed, not jaundiced, but cloudy, like something was dimming from the inside out.

And still he was never alone. The girls stayed close, never far from him. Surrounded by family and friends, he was bathed in love during his final days.

N.K.S would sit by his side and gently feed him, coaxing him, "Just one more bite for me, Baba… please?" Her voice soft, hopeful, trying to tether him to life through love. T.K.S followed him everywhere, shadowing him with quiet watchfulness, afraid to miss a second, afraid to let him disappear even for a moment. They didn't know how to handle death. They just knew how to love him. And somehow, that was enough.

He hated being shadowed. Even in his final days, Diaa clung fiercely to his independence. He didn't want people hovering over him. He'd grow irritated, saying things like, "I don't want Zozo to stay with me, she follows me everywhere." But even with that resistance, he couldn't hide his need for comfort.

Zozo once told me something that broke my heart open. She said that when he was tired, when the pain was bad or the silence too loud, he would take out his phone and check my location. And the moment he saw I was on my way home, his face would light up, his mood would change completely, like a child who finally knows his mother is near.

I was his safe place. He never said it out loud. He didn't need to.

He refused to use the walker and fought with us when we tried to make him use it, the only thing he would use without resistance was his cane, the only symbol of help that didn't offend his pride.

But the days continued to slip away. And the hospice nurse began to say what we were all too afraid to hear: "It won't be long now."

Then all at once. He began choking on water, unable to swallow unless he stood upright. His cognitive clarity would drift in and out, his gaze distant, his sentences sometimes unfinished. It felt like he was already living between worlds. Less here with us more somewhere else. Somewhere only he could see.

It was Sunday when I got the call. My daughter's voice was trembling on the other end of the line. They had tried to help him out of bed, but something popped, and the pain suddenly intensified. I immediately called hospice, and they sent the on-call nurse. After examining him, she said the words I had hoped I'd never hear again: "He needs to go to the hospital."

I told her to call the ambulance. Then I rushed to leave work, waiting only until my replacement arrived. As soon as they were ten minutes from the pharmacy, I left and drove to the hospital.

Inside, I found Zozo. She was waiting beside his stretcher. "They've taken him for X-rays," she told me. The results came back: everything looked normal. No fractures, no dislocation, no visible cause for his pain, just the cruel mystery of a body slowly shutting down. We were sent back home.

At that time, my brother was between jobs, and he started to sleep over, helping in quiet ways. But even with the extra help, Diaa was becoming more confused, slipping further away from us.

Friends visited every night, surrounding him with love, laughter, and shared memories. And one night, when the house was full of our closest friends, we saw it happen again. He was having an argument with someone we couldn't see, his hands moving, lips whispering words we couldn't hear, caught in that invisible world where he now spent most of his time.

Then, suddenly, his voice came back. Clear and deliberate. He looked up, pointed right at me, and said: "Because of her."

We all fell silent. At that moment, we knew. He was still fighting, not for himself, but because of me. He didn't want to leave because of me.

And then, just like that, he faded again.

It was the last time I heard his voice and the first time I allowed myself to cry in front of him. I had been strong for so long, always hiding my pain to protect him. But that night, I broke. Quiet tears spilled down my face, and he came back from wherever he went. He looked at me with the kindest eyes, the kind only he had and asked, "Why are you crying?"

I lied. I said, "My stomach hurts."

He nodded, accepted that kissed my lips and then he slipped back into silence, into that invisible realm he was already becoming part of.

Later, I sat by his side, knowing it was time. I had to tell him, gently, as his breathing grew more distant: "You walked through this world like an angel in disguise, quietly healing, lifting others, and loving without limits. You've done more good than most do in a lifetime."

And then I gave him what I knew he needed, what I had resisted for so long. The Permission to go.

"It's okay for you to leave now," I said. "I'll be fine. I always am."

For the first time, I meant it. Not because it was true but because he needed to hear it.

During the last week of his life, Diaa became restless, stubborn, and agitated. He kept saying he wanted to go to work or fix the car. One time, he actually left the house, and my brother walked outside with him before gently guiding him back in.

He couldn't stay in one position for more than five minutes. And I was utterly exhausted. One night, he fell asleep on the sofa, and I lay on the other one, positioned so that my face would be visible to him if he woke up.

I must have closed my eyes for just a moment. But when I opened them, he was gone.

I looked toward the front door; it didn't look open. Then a sudden breeze moved it just slightly. And that's when I saw him, on the ground, wearing only a shirt, no pants, in the freezing cold.

I ran to him, screaming for help. My brother and Alex rushed to scoop him off the cold concrete and wrapped him in a blanket.

Later, I checked the Ring camera footage, and my heart shattered. He had gone outside to throw away a dirty diaper, something he did to so I could continue to sleep. Or a final act of independence, I don't know. All I know is that he had been lying there, on the ground, for forty-five minutes before I woke up.

To this day, that moment haunts me. The image of his face, his hand reaching out, is seared into my soul. I don't know if I will ever forgive myself.

The next day, it happened again. He fell again while I closed my eyes and we called hospice to bring a hospital bed with rails, something that would keep him safe.

During that week the nurse came daily. His body was sore, and every movement hurt. I knew we were running out of time. I didn't know what to do, but then I knew. His family needed to say goodbye. So, I texted them and told them, "He can't talk anymore, but he can hear you. Talk to him one by one and say your goodbyes." I placed EarPods gently in his ears as they called, one after another, for over an hour, each voice crossing the distance, each one offering their final words, each one saying goodbye. When the last call ended, I sat beside him and held his hand.

"Diaa," I whispered, "if you can hear me, blink."

And he did.

I smiled through the tears. "You know how much I love you?" I asked softly.

He blinked again.

"And I know you love me too," I said, my voice trembling. "But I want to ask you for one thing." I leaned closer, my forehead almost touching his. "I need you to send me a message from wherever you are. Just one. Let me know that you're okay. I don't know how you'll do it, but you will. I believe you will."

And he blinked again. Slow. Certain. Deliberate.

A silent promise between two souls who would always find each other, no matter the distance.

As the weekend approached, Diaa's oxygen levels began to drop. I checked the machine, it wasn't working. Even the emergency oxygen tank was empty. I was furious. How could this happen now? So, I did what I do best: I started calling, nonstop, relentless, refusing to be ignored until a new oxygen machine and a full tank finally arrived. Slowly, his breathing began to stabilize.

But then he started to get hiccups. Something in me knew. I panicked. I ran to the bedroom, hiding the tears that had held on for so long.

That's when my brother followed me in, looked me in the eyes, and said gently, "This time is not about you. It's about your husband. Go and hold his hand, like you've done all along."

I wiped my tears. I gathered what was left of my strength. And returned to Diaa's side.

E.K was there, already holding his hand, her quiet sobs falling like rain on the sheets. I slipped my hand into his other one, never wanting to let go.

Later, when we were all too exhausted to speak, his ex-wife came and sat beside him too, sharing the silence, sharing the love, staying by his side as the final hours drew near.

Monday, December 2nd.

I was trying to get a reading on his oxygen levels, but the sensor wouldn't pick up anything. I tried it on myself, it worked fine. But on his finger, there was no reading.

Right then, his favorite hospice nurse called, saying she'd be at the house around two in the afternoon. I told her what was happening. She replied gently, "I'm on my way."

When she arrived, she walked straight to his bedside, her voice soft but firm: "What happened, my friend? Last Friday, you walked me to my car. I told you I was going on vacation for a week; don't you dare leave while I'm gone." Then, as if speaking to his soul, she kept asking, "Were you waiting for me?"

She took me outside. Her face was kind, but her words were steady and clear. "It's almost time," she said softly. "He has until tonight... maybe tomorrow morning."

My heart was pounding, caught between two impossible choices. I looked at her and asked, "Do I have time to run to the bank?"

I needed to pay the funeral home in advance. As a Muslim, I knew what this meant, he would need to be buried the same day or by the next morning. Everything had to be ready. It was my responsibility to honor him, to prepare, to do it right.

But how could I leave? Every cell in my body screamed stay. But I also knew that if I didn't go now, I might not be able to fulfill the final obligation he deserved.

She looked at me with understanding and nodded. "Yes. You still have time."

So, I left. I didn't even say goodbye; I didn't kiss him before I left like I did every day we were together. I left Torn, terrified, and full of dread. Praying that he would wait just a little longer. Praying that he knew I wasn't abandoning him, I was honoring him.

On the way to the bank, I tried to take the fastest route, cutting through back roads to save every precious second. But in my haze of fear and confusion, I got lost. Nothing looked familiar. Every turn felt wrong. I was fighting time, panicking, trying to reorient myself while driving forward.

When I finally reached the bank, I waited impatiently in line, the weight of every passing second crushing me.

And then my phone lit up. Notification after notification from the doorbell camera.

I knew. I knew something had happened. I felt it in my chest before I even looked at the screen.

He was gone.

He waited for the moment I left to take his last breath.

And now, looking back, I know why. He wanted to spare me the pain. He was still trying to protect me, even in death. He knew that if I had been in the room, I would never recover from watching the light leave his eyes. He didn't want that memory burned into me. He wanted my last image of him to be alive, even if barely.

That was Diaa. My guardian. My love.

Even in his final act, he gave me the gift of being spared while he bore the weight of goodbye alone.

Chapter 25: Is This Woman Really Me?

Is this woman really me?

I stare at my reflection, not just in mirrors, but in the pharmacy's glass doors, in every polished surface that catches my image when I am not prepared. The face looking back is glowing, almost radiant, untouched by time. It shows no trail of the tears I've shed, no shadow of the nights I have spent awake, no outward sign of grief. My skin is smooth. My smile is inviting. My eyes know the truth, but they too are determined to keep my secret. Every feature on my face is complicit in hiding my scars, my pain.

Is this woman really me?

I have walked through fire. I have lost and rebuilt, lost again, and somehow kept breathing. To a stranger I might look like any other woman. pleasant, even beautiful, but no one would ever guess the storms that have passed through me. Sometimes I can't believe it myself. Sometimes I look at myself and whisper: why? Why does my face tell a different story than my heart? Why does it lie so easily?

It has been one year and four months since you left me. One year and four months since my heart was ripped out of my chest and left beating somewhere I can no longer reach. I did not choose this life, this hollow space where my pulse used to be. With you beside me, I never thought about the future, whatever came, we faced it together. Now the days stretch ahead like a road without signs, a path I am forced to walk alone.

Sometimes, when the world is noisy, when laughter or work fills the air, it almost feels okay to breathe. I smile, even laugh, and for a moment I believe I am living. But the instant I am alone, the silence hits me like a fist. Your absence turns into a physical pain, an invisible hand that grips my heart and squeezes until my chest tightens and my eyes brim with tears that refuse to fall. In those moments I catch myself secretly hoping the tightening will deepen and linger long enough to become a doorway leading me back to you.

I look for signs that you didn't leave me behind. I watch the rain fall and imagine it as a shimmering portal, a thin curtain between this world and yours. If I can just reach it in time before it closes, maybe it will take me to you. I speed my steps, my heartbeat quickens, always hoping I'll make it in time, but never do.

A few days before you died, I told you that you had done amazingly in this lifetime, that you had passed every trial with humility and grace. I needed you to know how much I loved you. You blinked, telling me you already knew. But I had one more request, one last act of love.

I asked you to let me know that you were okay in the spirit realm. In my heart I had no doubt you had passed the tests of this life with excellence. You were dignified in everything you did, and even more dignified in sickness and in pain. That alone secured your place in heaven. But still, I needed you to promise. I needed to stay connected to you even after death, to be loved by you even after death. And as impossible as it seems, you didn't let me down. With one slow blink you said yes. You promised you would find a way.

You passed away on December 2nd, 2024. One month to the day after the girls arrived on November 2nd. That alone felt like your final gift, waiting for them, making sure I would not be alone, and then letting go exactly one month later, as if even your departure was deliberate, measured, an act of love.

Two days after you left, my immigration case long buried under disappointment, moved. I applied for an immigrant visa through my employer in 2022 and under the fog of everything that followed I forgot about it. The Labor PERM Certificate, the crucial first step, the key to the entire journey, had been approved. Certified on December 4th. Two days after you passed.

I didn't check my email until the last week of December. And there it was, an email from the lawyer, just words on a screen, yet it felt like a pulse from another world.

Was that your doing? Did you make that happen? Did you somehow reach forward, knowing this would become my only path to legal status, to staying in the life we built together? Was it Irony or divine intervention or are you keeping your promise from the other side. I cannot say with certainty. But I know the timing. And I know you.

Almost three weeks had passed since you left, and still there was silence. No dream. No flicker. No whisper. Just a hollow ache. Everyone important had called to share visions of you, dreams, signs, something from the other side. Everyone but me. I had nothing.

I remember driving with our daughter Nat.K when the weight inside me broke. For the first time I said the words out loud: I feel so guilty.

That last week of your life had drained every ounce of me. You were restless and agitated, unable to sit still more than five minutes at a time. For days I barely slept, my body stiff with vigilance, until finally exhaustion conquered me. And in that exhaustion, I failed to be there when you needed me. You fell. Twice. And both times I was asleep.

I felt guilty.

The kind of guilt that cuts deeper than any wound. Did the falls speed up your end? If I had just stayed awake longer, if I had pushed through the exhaustion one more hour, maybe we would have had more time together.

And I felt guilty for leaving your side at the end regardless of the reason, regardless of what the nurse told me, regardless of what I have told myself since. I know you may have chosen that moment to spare me. I know you loved me enough to do that. But I also know that I could have stayed. I could have pushed through. I could have held your hand one last time. I didn't say goodbye; I didn't kiss you before I left like I every day we were together

I have never said these words before. Even now, I don't know if I forgive myself. But I hope you do.

That night, your picture sat on my nightstand, the same photo I had been touching like a talisman for days. Suddenly the anger poured out. I started yelling at you at a photograph. I reminded you of the promise you made, of how I was still waiting for the message you had agreed to send me. My voice cracked as I said that everyone had been getting messages from you but me. I wanted mine. I wanted my proof.

Then the anger passed. My voice softened. I said goodnight, my love. I told you I was going to sleep. And then I picked up my phone and opened TikTok, the way millions of people do at the end of an ordinary night.

And then you answered.

A video played. The voice on the screen said:

"Your deceased loved one wants to tell you… As my life was coming to an end, my health was in a very bad state, and I was suffering greatly inside. I didn't want you to see me like that. But I believe my departure was the right decision. Now I finally feel at peace and am no longer tormented by pain… Please do not blame yourself for my death. It was not your fault. Even though I have left this world, my soul is still with you and will never leave you. No matter where I am, I will always be with you. Forever."

I don't know if it was the algorithm or something more. But for me, that was the message you promised me. You heard every word I had said. You answered the exact guilt I had been carrying in silence for weeks. I laughed and cried at the same time. I saved the video, played it over and over. I shared it with everyone. It was you making good on your promise. It was you telling me everything I needed to hear and most importantly, telling me that you were okay.

But that was not the only sign.

One night I asked you to visit me in a dream, not the kind you forget as soon as you open your eyes, but a dream I could hold onto, one I could keep like a photograph. That night you came.

It wasn't a blur. It was a full day, vivid and real. We woke up together in the soft morning light, and for the first time in months your face was rested, your body strong and I could hug you without being afraid of breaking a bone. So, I hugged you so hard and for as long as I could. We made breakfast the way we used to, you butter the toast while I poured the coffee. We laughed about nothing, small inside jokes no one else would understand. Later, we walked through a mall, wandering from shop to shop without hurry, your hand warm in mine, your voice easy. In the afternoon we drove up winding roads to visit your friends at their new house, a home on a green hill surrounded by mountains, a lake shimmering at its foot like glass. I remember standing with you on the deck, breathing in the clean air, telling you we should buy a house there. You smiled, nodded, and for a moment the future felt possible again. Then, as the day began to fade, you placed your hand on your chest and said you were feeling tired and wanted to go back home. And just like that, I woke. But I remembered everything, the warmth, the touch, the laughter, the smell of coffee as if I had truly been given one more day with you.

In March it was my first birthday without you, and my fiftieth. It was supposed to be the milestone we had planned to celebrate with a vacation, a trip we had built in our minds as a small escape into joy. Instead, there was no vacation. There was no you. I was cracked open with grief, and when the day came it felt like another weight pressing me down. I didn't dress up. No cake. No candles. Just the quiet heaviness of an existence in a world you no longer walk.

Then in April, on an ordinary day driving home, I was remembering your eyes, your eyebrows, the way you looked at me as if I were the only person who mattered on earth. While I was lost in that memory, Siri interrupted: "My love is calling you." Your name appeared on the car screen. My brain froze. Your phone was with me in a locked, zippered pocket in my bag, and for a heartbeat I thought if I answered, I would hear your voice at the other end. But my reflexes were slow, and by the time I pressed accept, the call had stopped.

The radio came back on. And this time it was playing "Hey Shorty, It's Your Birthday" the song we had played for you on your own fiftieth birthday. That was no coincidence.

There was no denying it was you. You came to celebrate my birthday. You didn't forget about me.

I cried and yelled and then talked to you all the way home, my hands gripping the steering wheel like a lifeline. I called everyone again to tell them how you had reached out, how you had found a way to let me know you were with me even now, especially on a milestone that was supposed to be ours.

But lately, the signs have gone quiet.

I don't see you as often in my dreams anymore. No messages. No flickering lights. No songs on the radio at the exact right moment. The silence has returned, and it is a different kind of silence than before, not the fresh silence of loss, but something older, more settled, and somehow harder to bear.

Did you move on? Did you forget me? Or is it what I read somewhere that you don't miss me because you have access to me. That you can see me, even when I cannot see you. That the distance only runs one way.

I want to believe that. I am trying to believe that.

But how do I move on when the mention of your name pulls tears into my eyes without permission? Not sometimes. Every time. Without warning. Without consent. Your name lands in a room and something in my chest opens before I can stop it.

I don't know how to grieve someone I am not finished loving. I don't know how to move forward when every step feels like a step away from you. Maybe that is not what moving on means. Maybe moving on doesn't mean leaving you behind. Maybe it just means learning to carry you differently, less like a wound, more like a scar. Still there. Still yours. But no longer bleeding.

Now, it is setting in.

I am fifty years old and alone. What now? If I live to be as old as my mother, that is over thirty more years. Am I going to grow old alone? Will I ever find love again? Or have you ruined all men for me because we were too perfect to be true, and men will fall short in comparison?

Will I ever find a new kind of love where I can still open my heart to a good person without erasing your legacy? Or was your touch the last touch I will ever feel?

What will happen to me with all the immigration changes? Will I be forced to leave the life I built with you and abandon all these memories? I can't drive downtown without feeling the oxygen sucked from my lungs, because we drove on that road together. It happens on every street we passed on together; every route lined with the ghosts of our life. I wanted that pain because it was a reminder that you were here, and our love was real.

People are no longer showing up. E.K doesn't want to come over because she can't bear that you're not there. Alex moved to New York, and Zozo followed him. Everyone has moved on. But I feel stuck.

Life is different now. I don't know how to be a mother again. You fought to bring the girls here. You didn't want to leave without making sure I had someone to take care of me. But I have been caring for everyone for as long as I can remember. I don't know how to accept that I need help. I don't know how to be a hands-on mother, after so many years of mothering from a distance. Now that they are here, I don't know what is best for them or if I even have a say in their lives. For a while I struggled because part of me felt that their presence was paid for with your life and it wasn't a price I would ever choose to pay. I would have accepted being away from them knowing you would be with me.

I look in the mirror and see my face, familiar, yet almost foreign. The same eyes, the same skin, but nothing feels like me. I tilt my head, searching for a sign of the woman I once was.

Is this woman really me?

A face unscathed, a face with no sign of struggle, while everything inside me screams that I am broken. How can a face stay so calm when the soul behind it is torn? How can skin be smooth when grief has carved deep canyons inside my chest?

I lean closer.

Is this woman really me?

Will I continue to fight for my survival, to keep standing up, or will I throw in the towel and let life break me again? Will I always be in between, neither the weak, broken woman from my past nor the fulfilled woman I was with you?

I don't have the answers. I whisper them to the mirror anyway, like a prayer or a dare. What are you made of now? What's left of you? Can you still become something new? The silence doesn't answer, but the woman in the mirror doesn't look away either.

All I know is that if I can just keep smiling, even a small smile or if I can make someone else smile, then that is a good day. Maybe that's what survival is. Maybe that's how healing is. One tiny moment of light inside the dark.

One day at a time. One smile at a time. One breath at a time.

And just like that, maybe, the woman looking back at me from the mirror, the one with the unscarred face but the scarred heart will become me. Not the woman I was. Not the woman I lost. But someone entirely new.

I used to think strength meant being unbreakable. I used to think it meant never showing the cracks, never letting anyone see you falter. I spent years believing that if I could just hold it together on the outside, I was strong.

But I know better now.

You don't have to be a superhero to be strong. Sometimes strength is just waking up. Getting dressed when your body wants to stay in bed. Smiling at someone even when the smile costs you something. Putting one foot in front of the other on a road you never asked to walk.

And sometimes, without knowing it, that is enough. More than enough. You start to inspire people, you give hope and you set an example on how to stand up and face life regardless of how many blows it sends your way.

You inspire them by existing. By surviving. By refusing, even on the hardest days, to disappear. By refusing to stay down when everyone expects you to.

I didn't know that about myself until recently. I still don't fully believe it. But I am beginning to.

Grief does not end. It reshapes us.

Love does not die. It changes form.

I once thought survival meant returning to who I used to be, but I know now it means becoming someone I have never been before. I carry you with me in the silence, in the laughter I manage to share, in the steps I force myself to take one day at a time.

If life has taught me anything, it is that brokenness and beauty can live inside the same body, and that even in the hollow space where loss resides, love still finds a way to breathe.